BIOTECHNOLOGY
ENTREPRENEURSHIP
From Science to Solutions

Michael L. Salgaller, PhD

**LOGOS
PRESS**

BIOTECHNOLOGY ENTREPRENEURSHIP
From Science to Solutions
Michael L. Salgaller, PhD

Published in The United States of America
by
Logos Press®, Washington DC
www.Logos-Press.com
info@Logos-Press.com

10 9 8 7 6 5 4 3 2

ISBN-13
Hardcover: 978-1-934899-13-7
Softcover: 978-1-934899-14-4

Library of Congress Cataloging-in-Publication Data

1006479295

Biotechnology entrepreneurship : from science to solutions / [edited by] Michael L. Salgaller.
p. cm.
Includes bibliographical references and index.
ISBN 978-1-934899-13-7 (case bound : alk. paper) -- ISBN 978-1-934899-14-4 (perfect bound : alk. paper)
1. Biotechnology industries--Management. 2. Entrepreneurship. 3. New business enterprises. I. Salgaller, Michael L.
HD9999.B442B569 2010
660.6068'4--dc22
2010027702

Contents

To my wife, Lauren, and son, Grant - whomst I love

Author Contact Information

Chapter 1
Michael L. Salgaller, PhD
1027 Wintergreen Terrace
Rockville, MD 20850
Tel: 301-601-5789
mlsalgaller@yahoo.com

Chapter 2
Shalom Leaf, JD
Attorney at Law, Shalom Leaf, PC
600 Madison Avenue, 22nd Floor
New York, NY 10022
Tel: 212-355-4390   Fax: 917-210-3748
sleaf@leaflegal.com

Chapter 3
Henry Miller
SVP & Global Practice Head, SPG Life Sciences Executive Search
630 Freedom Business Center, 3rd Floor
King of Prussia, PA 19406
Tel: 610-768-7766   Fax: 610 768 7701
hmiller@spges.com

Chapter 4
Nancy W. Vensko, JD
Partner, Fitch, Even, Tabin & Flannery
1010 Peach Street
San Luis Obispo, CA 93401
Tel: 805-541-2800   Fax: 805-541-2802
nvensko@fitcheven.com

Chapter 5
Chris Copple, PhD
CEO, Starise Ventures
12308 Piney Glen Lane
Potomac, MD 20854
Tel: 240-602-1416
starise.ventures@verizon.net

Chapter 6
Bethany Mancilla, MBA
Vice-President, Business Development and Alliance Management, Micromet AG, Inc.
6707 Democracy Boulevard, Suite 505
Bethesda, Maryland 20817
Tel: 240-752-1420
bethany.mancilla@gmail.com

CHAPTER 7
Steven M. Ferguson, CLP
Deputy Director, Licensing & Entrepreneurship,
Office of Technology Transfer, National Institutes of Health
6011 Executive Boulevard, Suite 325
Rockville, MD 20852
Tel: 301-435-5561   Fax: 301-402-0220
FERGUSOS@od6100m1.od.nih.gov

Ruchika Nijhara, PhD, MBA
Senior Licensing Manager, Office of Technology Commercialization
Georgetown University
Harris Building, Suite 1500
3300 Whitehaven Street, NW Washington, D.C. 20007
Tel: 202-687-3721   Fax: 202-687-3111
rn86@georgetown.edu

CHAPTER 8
Libbie Mansell, PhD, MBA, RAC
President, White Oak BioPharma Solutions, LLC
21624 Ripplemead Drive, Suite 100
Gaithersburg, MD 20882
Tel: 240-855-2323
lmansell@whiteoak-biopharma.com

CHAPTER 9
Rhonda Greenapple, MSPH
President, Reimbursement Intelligence. LLC
2 Shunpike Rd., Third Floor
Madison, NJ 07940
Tel: 973-805-2301   Fax: 973-377-7930
RGreenapple@radicalgrp.com

CHAPTER 10
James Hawkins, PhD, MBA
Managing Director, FOCUS Securities, LLC
1133 20th Street, NW, Suite 200
Washington , DC 20036
Tel: 202-470-1971   Fax: 202-785-9413
jim.hawkins@focusbankers.com

CHAPTER 11
Susan K. Finston
President, Finston Consulting, LLC
1101 Pennsylvania Ave., NW, Suite 600
Washington, DC 20004
Tel: 202-756-7749   Fax: 202-330-5550
susan@finstonconsulting.com

CHAPTER 1

Why Start a Biotechnology Company?

Michael L. Salgaller, PhD
Biotechnology Entrepreneur, Venture Capitalist, and Medical Researcher

S tarting a biotechnology company is quite likely the most important, most rewarding, most difficult undertaking of your professional career. It will bring you unparalleled moments of accomplishment and success—surrounded on both sides with a healthy dose of doubt and uncertainty. It is a very long road, measured in years rather than months. And it is much easier to achieve satisfaction than success—although the goal is to achieve both.

But why start a company? Businessmen and financiers will tell you the correct answer is: to make money. However, there are those who would contend that people become scientists because they either do not care about making money, or they do not understand the practical value of being able to buy things—even if they do not need them. I know hundreds and hundreds of scientists, and I cannot recall any of them ever saying they got into research so they could retire by the time they were fifty. I am not saying that money is not even on our radar screen; it is just not the major driver telling the planes where to go. Things like finding out something previously undiscovered or unknown are more important than the pursuit and vestiges of affluence. The main point of research is asking questions—not finding answers, because those answers simply lead to more questions. Being a scientific researcher means having intellectual ADHD, and going off in unanticipated directions built into your career path. The challenge arises when you realize that one of those tangents is worth pursuing for a longer, straighter direction than the others, and you realize that your university, medical center, or foundation, can only take you so far. All of a sudden, you are Dorothy at the edge of Munchkin Land; the yellow brick road is long and winding, its destination uncertain. In the world of biotechnology entrepreneurship, you have got to be able to convince yourself and others that there's a pot of gold at the end of this particular rainbow.

Of course, there is so much more to starting a biotechnology company than the money. Biotechnology has had, and will continue to have, tremendous impact on society. It has the potential to extend lives, to better the quality of life for those afflicted, and to prevent a disease from even getting started. In these ways and many others, starting a biotechnology company can be more rewarding than other entrepreneurial pursuits, such as opening a restaurant or developing software. There is something exciting, something motivating, about coming up with a solution no one else has done. And others—even those who cannot define biotechnology and find it mysterious—find it thrilling as well. If you have any doubts, test it out next time you are at any get-together where people ask one another what they do or what they are up to. Tell them you are starting a company to treat disease X or prevent disease Y, and the majority of reactions will be positive and impressed. Sadly but realistically, the majority of dire diseases are conversation-starters. Cancer, for example, is not unlike other topics whose familiarity quickly establishes a common bond.

Of course, the long and challenging path of biotechnology entrepreneurship is not undertaken for the impression you make, or for social comfort and ease of interaction. However, such reactions underscore and emphasize the importance of the undertaking. As previously mentioned, it is well within the realm of possibility that starting a biotechnology company will be the most important, most rewarding thing you do in your career.

So, this pursuit can—and should—bring personal satisfaction in alignment with the financial opportunity. And it is not crucial to determine the order you should put these two items, or the weight each is given when compared to the other. Instead, it is more important to point out that, if you do not at least recognize the monetary component of what you are doing, you understand that there are other avenues to your goal that do not require starting a company. One option is to stay at the university, hospital, or research center in which you are currently employed, and to hand the technology to someone else to develop. In this way, the technology moves forward, out of the lab, and it is up to someone else to focus on the financial issues and rewards involved of getting to the people who need it. Or, instead of becoming an entrepreneur, you could work with your technology transfer or licensing office to hand it off to an existing company. Although you can still remain involved to some extent, you will not have to focus on making money. If you would prefer to develop it yourself, then at least a threshold level of interest in making money becomes important. It is okay if you do not admit it to the outside world. After all, improving people's lives for financial gain may seem discomforting or disquieting. Yet the reality is that it will take a lot of money to develop your idea, and it is unlikely to make money for many years. Consequently, you will need outside resources to develop your technology. And I can assure you that *they* are interested in making money—even if you are not.

As will be discussed in several chapters on raising money, it is critical to have at least a familiarity with the business of biotechnology. Starting a company means investing your time, energy, and—in the majority of cases—money. You should know at least as much about this type of investment as any mutual fund or retirement account with which you are involved. This need is compounded if the entrepreneur has a family who will be impacted by the decision to start a company. Entrepreneurship should result from family discussions about its impact. It is a highly risky career move, especially if you already have a position. Given the volatility of biotechnology as a career, this is not to say that staying put is not without risk— but at least you know where your next paycheck is coming from. If you strike out on your own, it could be quite some time before you again draw a regular paycheck. Some areas of biotechnology—such as medical devices and the development of diagnostic kits—may generate revenues within a few years of company inception. If your business model is fee-for-service or contract service—such as charging others for access to your technology—you may generate revenues within the first year of company inception. However, initial returns will be modest and, as with any other business, should be plowed back into the business. If you are fortunate enough to attract outside financing, providing a salary to the founders is not a top priority of investors, as it does little to move the company forward and increase its value. Though your academic colleagues will tell you that "tenure is not what it used to be," as was previously mentioned, at least it is one way to have a regular paycheck—even if it is not the guaranteed appointment-for-life that it used to be.

Many entrepreneurs stay at their present positions even after company inception, incorporation, and onset of dedicated activities. This is usually because of financial dependency on one's current position. This path is understandable given the uncertainties of company formation, and the need for some maintenance of one's current position in case the company does not make it. After all, (academic) tenured positions or (industry) senior management positions can be hard to get. And it is unlikely one can return to a former position after resignation. Still, although it seems obvious that one cannot do two jobs, entrepreneurs often try: keeping their current appointment while trying to get their new project off the ground. Not surprisingly, the result is often that insufficient attention and energy is devoted to the new company. If this insufficient attention and energy becomes a chronic situation, it can lead to what is referred to as the "walking dead;" an entrepreneur who has had a company for years— but has seen little or no progress on either the financial or technical front. There are ways to avoid becoming the walking dead—as will be discussed in Chapter 5

There does not seem to be one particular personality type when it comes to biotechnology entrepreneurs. Some appear brash and confident, enthusiastic and emotional when discussing their company. Some are surprisingly unassuming and reserved, given the importance of selling oneself and marketing one's ideas. Regardless of personality, you as entrepreneur will need to be comfortable leaving your comfort zone. You have likely achieved some measure of recognition in your field, along with a measure of accomplishment. In your mind, this recognition and accomplishment is sufficient to believe that people are willing to back either your ideas, or those of others that you will commercialize for them. Therefore, there is—and should be—some threshold level of confidence that one can succeed. It does not take supreme confidence or ego to start a company—but it does take belief in one's own ability. There is no way you can get others to support (financially, emotionally, or otherwise) your undertaking if you do not truly believe in it. If you do not believe your company will succeed, stay at your current position. Even if you want to stay at your current position and let someone else take your ideas forward in your place (via licensing from your entity to the start-up), do not move forward until and unless you believe your ideas can be commercialized. Do not let others assume all the risk for an enterprise you do not believe in.

As an academic in an academic setting, you are playing a game in which you know the rules, regardless of how well you manage to play by them. As a medical researcher or other type of entrepreneur in the non- or not-for-profit sector, you have also been living the reality since your graduate career began. Now, the rules have changed; the game can be unfamiliar and unsettling.

Getting back to the topic of what you have accomplished in your career, starting your own company is also likely to be quite a humbling experience. If you have achieved any level of renown or notoriety, it is a humbling experience to suddenly be surrounded by and interacting with those who have no idea who you are or what you have done. Unless you are one of those rare scientists who is personally and professionally recognized by the lay public—in which case you are likely to have no trouble attracting support for your company—you need to sell, market, and advertise yourself and your ideas. You cannot let the work speak for itself—or else the work will be mute, and your company dead.

If you want to get an idea of what this lack of recognition is like—and especially if you doubt it pertains to you—take a look at any entertainment or gossip magazine from a foreign country. Those people praised and vilified on the cover are well-known local celebrities. However, outside of their countries, few would elicit interest—let alone name recognition. The same applies to you outside your field of expertise. Enjoy being mobbed, being the center of attention following your plenary lecture at some important professional conference? Enjoy keeping a running count of how many people say, "I've always wanted to meet you?" Then my advice is: stay where you are. Venturing outside your comfort zone is not just a challenge for the nerves, but the ego as well.

Another helpful, another favorable, characteristic of an entrepreneur is to stand tall and assured in the face of wilting criticism and doubt. Do not let defensiveness turn people away, or self-confidence turn to dismissiveness. Certainly, progressing through your scientific career involves continually running the gauntlet of opinion and derision. Whether it originates from the audience during discussions after a lecture, or anonymous reviewers critiquing an paper submission, facing criticism and doubt is standard operating procedure. Most scientists and researchers would contend, understandably, it is precisely such discourse and debate that leads to better ideas, better answers. It forces you to go back and re-evaluate, to look at the holes and deficiencies. Over time, as you become more professional in how you share your discoveries, you become more and more accomplished at anticipating the criticism. And, in turn, you become more and more accomplished at knowing how to overcome such criticism—whether that is by simple oral argument, or by actually amending the way a series of experiments are designed and performed. You are accustomed to comments from those who know—to at least some extent—of what they critique. Of course, there are those who enjoy hearing themselves talk; the sound of their own voices. There are those who seem to comment in *inverse* proportion to their understanding. Some are not particularly tactful about how they expressed themselves, or particularly concerned that they're not. However, at minimum, your work is being scorned or mocked by others with a scientific or technical background.

You need a unique backbone to put up with having your theories and ideas and ideals reviewed by those with solely a financial or business background, who have not taken a science course since freshman year in high school. Mix in a generous dose of those who believe that the case studies in business school are applicable to the real world—and what you have is commentary on your life's work by someone who's never actually started or run their own company. In many areas of work, this is not so unusual. After all, you do not have to be able to draw a straight line to be an art critic. You do not have to have the talent to boil water to be a food critic. And you could be highly allergic to popcorn and still be a movie critic. Allegedly, however, science is generally objective and art generally subjective. You are not supposed to hear, "I know what I like when I see it," when referring to a treatment, diagnostic, or device. But, in effect, you will.

Consequently, perseverance is an important tool in your arsenal—along with the ability to remain calm in the face of unrelenting, unrepentant stupidity and arrogance. For, if you keep faith that you have a way to effectively address a burden on the health of society, then one day you will connect with those who truly value what you have to offer. It may take one day or a thousand—but you have to believe that it will come. You have to believe more than just for you—but enough for those you want to invest; to put some chips into the game.

You also have to believe for your friends and—especially—your family. You will need the support of your family, sometimes literally. Raising an initial amount of money (capital) from family and friends to get your company off the ground is par for the course. You potentially face the challenge of having them both emotional and financially invested in your undertaking. As with any other significant career decision, anticipate the reaction ranging from blind support to complete dismissal. In this regard, having family and friends back up their support and faith with cold, hard cash is similar to most other entrepreneurial undertakings. That is, it is very high risk, and anyone financially involved should run—not walk— to the nearest attorney. With any investment, having the right legal framework protects both sides, and establishes ground rules. In the biotechnology arena, the long time-frames involved make a mutually agreeable legal structure especially important. Most potential investors know how quickly new businesses fail; a very high percentage within the first few years. However, biotechnology is a particularly thorny situation because it gets more complicated the longer an investor stays involved. With many investments, a successful company makes revenue after a year or two, soon followed by profit— and profit-sharing. In biotechnology, many companies exist for 5-7 years or more without generating any revenue—let alone profit. This is because of the lengthy approval process required by the Food and Drug Administration (and similar regulatory agencies around the world) before a product can be marketed and sold. It takes a lot of money to get a product to market, and so a biotechnology company is typically in a constant fund-raising mode. Long before the first in a series of professional investors (such as angel investors or seed-stage venture capital firms) decides to put money in, you should have informed your family and friends that the "new kids on the block" will not be respectful of their investment. In fact, they will likely see their investment as "dumb money;" bringing no value to the fledging company beyond the pure source of capital. Once professional investors ("smart money") enter the picture, family and friends are often show the proverbial door. Their participation with, and input to, the company is discouraged. Most materially, their investment is likely to be "crammed down"—the percentage ownership that came with a certain amount of investment decreases involuntarily on the part of the original investor. A cram-down is usually required of the new investor before any money is put in. So, biotechnology investing is uniquely strange in that, the more a successful the company, the more you may see your potential return go *down*! The new, smart money may also be willing to buy you out, making it financially attractive to be shown the door. Just keep in mind that they offer less than what something is truly worth. Consequently, family and friends investors may not get what they feel is a fair return.

In summary, avoid fractured families and devastated friendships: give all the facts and potential complications up front. Since there is a strong likelihood this will not be your good suit, get an expert (attorney, mentor, etc.) involved at the onset—and throughout the process. Better to bore your investors with minutiae than leave something out they might find riveting—or, at least, of interest. They need to generally aware of the long time-lines involved in bringing a life science product to market. No one—not even you—will have an idea of what kind of return they can expect or when they can expect it. This is not like opening a new restaurant, where you could gaze night after night over a room of happy diners and generate realistic financial projections. What kind of financial projections can you generate when you will not have any revenue for years, or be profitable for even longer? Calculating 3- or 5-year financial projections is something professional investors will require—yet will readily admit is slightly less accurate than picking lottery numbers. Nonetheless, you can still tap their motivation to invest, since it is likely similar to yours: the desire to actively contribute to the betterment of society in a tangible way.

Lastly, although others may invest and advise, your new company's team is you and your fellow founders. You need to wear many hats and coats (suit and lab, to start with). Are you good at delegating? Well, that skill will come in handy when your company gets its first major investment and expands. For now, being able to write and complete a strong, focused, time-line-filled to-do list is much more important. There is a saying: "a goal without a plan is a wish." The goal you have chosen is achievable, but without planning and preparation is might never be realized. One of your first goals was to learn more about the business of biotechnology entrepreneurship. So, continue on this goal and read on. Good luck!

Chapter 2

Company Formation and Organization

Shalom Leaf, JD
Attorney at Law, Shalom Leaf PC

INTRODUCTION: THE BIOTECH START-UP AND LEGAL COUNSEL

Congratulations! You are starting a new company. After carefully weighing the personal and business risks and benefits and after much soul searching and detailed planning, you have decided to leave the familiar confines of academia or working for others, to cast anchor and embark on a new biotech venture! You are in it for the long haul; developing and commercializing your company's products or services will be a protracted project, full of uncertainty and frustration, but the science and technology are replete with promise: ingenious, novel, intriguing, perhaps beautiful. Your company also has the potential to do a world of good, whether you will be fighting disease, ameliorating injury, or extending human life or capabilities. You respect, hopefully even admire, your co-venturers. If you are a wise entrepreneur, you have sorted out your roles, reached a business understanding, smoothed over any difficulties, and are positively bonding—while building on each other's team spirit and enthusiasm. You are even—perhaps especially—looking forward to expanding your personal range and becoming a businessman, a company founder, a successful entrepreneur. Business cannot be as difficult as science, can it? You pick up the buzzwords immediately—soon you are speaking the language and well on your way to fluency. And, if the technology works, and the company realizes its potential to save or improve human life, another wellspring of satisfaction will likely gush up before your very eyes: you will be rich—or at least *richer*; rewarded with the kind of satisfaction few can achieve or understand.

You are aware that these reveries are selective, but they're positive, good for morale, motivating, energizing. You float along buoyantly in their wake, until the day you and your partners show up for a meeting in a downtown conference room. Some suits or deliberately business-casual types walk in and start pestering you with doubts, questions, contingencies, minutiae, limitations, rules, equivocations, convoluted phrases, arcane terminology, evasive analyses, qualifications heaped on qualifications. Suddenly, you are not having a great time, and the worst of it is, it is going to cost you time and money. A lot.

Unfortunately, the scenario we have just depicted, like so many types or stereotypes, all too often represents an aspect of reality; in this case, the experience—or a portion of the experience—of many new biotech entrepreneurs. There's not much point, especially in this brief chapter, in sorting out the whys and wherefores or the blame. Some lawyers deserve their negative reviews. For better or worse, the law pervades our culture; the businessman who badmouths lawyers and bemoans their fees is often the first to pick up the phone to demand a cease-and-desist letter. Biotech entrepreneurs who find themselves in these situations, or who anticipate them, have a number of typical coping mechanisms: avoidance, condescension, and a do-it-yourself approach being prominent among them.

This purpose of this chapter is to outline, as completely as possible in a very short discussion, some of the legal basics of organizing a biotech company, and to point out along the way some of the typical mistakes that founders make. A disclaimer at this point: this summary is intended for general informational purposes, not legal advice. It is necessarily incomplete—books have been written about each of the issues touched upon—and it does not address your individual situation. You should, of course, consult with competent counsel about the matters discussed. This disclaimer, like the aforementioned scenario, introduces a couple of anterior issues that are, in practice, all too often overlooked or casually addressed. How does one go about hiring a biotech start-up lawyer? How best to think about the lawyer's role?

Of course, the two issues are closely linked. We believe that legal requirements are not external to the start-up's business, but integral to its success. Lawyers are not, or should not be, expensive or unscrupulous—nor should they be unwelcome exterminators of troublesome issues. Rather, they should be valued advisors and business partners who help create and protect key business assets. While legal knowledge and skills are paramount, some lawyers are also well-connected and able to introduce their start-up clients to potential financing sources, business partners, and other professionals. Like other key participants, counsel should be retained at an early stage (preferably *at the very outset*), and the founders should have a clear understanding as to the costs involved and the value that's being provided. Too often, founders delay hiring expert counsel and find themselves paying extra to undo mistakes—or worse, find that the mistakes (for example, unwise agreements among founders or the use of potentially infringing trademarks) are difficult and costly to undo.

How does one select a lawyer? Founders often give too much weight to expense or reputation. A number of times, I have had the uncomfortable experience of representing a major research university in a negotiation with a start-up biotech represented by an enthusiastic, but fairly clueless, general practice/corporate attorney. At the opposite extreme, I have found myself negotiating with a partner at a major firm and a senior associate (accompanied by their silent companion, the junior), representing a poor (and soon to be poorer!) biotech. Because most biotech companies require knowledgeable counsel in corporate, tax, patent, and FDA areas, among others, a well-known mega-firm is often the choice by default, despite the generally high rates involved. There are, however, sophisticated attorneys who practice in medium-sized or small firm settings and, in an era of electronic accessibility, there is less value than previously existed in having "a partner down the hall" as opposed to "a colleague at another firm."

Such suggestions are not meant to recommend a particular type of firm, but rather to suggest a thoughtful and balanced process. Founders should make a careful decision after networking and seeking referrals from colleagues, other entrepreneurs, university contacts (*e.g.*, at tech transfer offices or business schools). Candidate firms may also come from those who sponsor and attend life science networking/informational events. In addition to being reliable and discerning, the referrer will ideally have had a professional relationship with the attorney in a biotech start-up situation, or in an engagement requiring similar knowledge and skills. Prospective counsel should be interviewed and willingly answer questions about their background and experience. Issues of cost, staffing, and level of service should be addressed proactively, in relation to both the initial retention and subsequent decisions about the management of transactions, litigation, and other matters. My personal belief is that many companies will be best served by having a primary attorney (often, but not necessarily, a corporate attorney) whom the founders trust and are comfortable with, is responsive and personally involved in the legal work for the company, and is an excellent communicator and "translator," able to coordinate the legal work of the company (whether at the same or different firms), to the extent needed. Many attorneys will say they are interested in growing with you—in the hopes of increasing the number of billable hours as your biotech progresses. Instead, as previously mentioned, find a person or practice willing to *facilitate* your growth and development. Such willingness is a key selection factor the entrepreneur should use. In fact, many entrepreneurs do not realize that—just as with investors—lawyers should bring "value-add" to the table. An attorney or firm willing to play an active role in your company's growth and development separates them from the pack, and should be a major consideration when selecting legal counsel.

CHOICE OF ENTITY; JURISDICTION OF FORMATION OR INCORPORATION

Recent years have witnessed a proliferation of new entity types, however biotech start-ups will generally consider three options:

- A limited liability company (LLC)
- A corporation that has elected under Subchapter "S" of the Internal Revenue Code to be treated as a partnership for tax purposes (S Corp)
- An ordinary, garden-variety corporation that has not made such an election and is therefore taxed on an entity level under Subchapter "C" of the Internal Revenue Code (C Corp)

While these entities differ from one another in many ways, two sets of factors are crucial in determining choice of entity: tax treatment and investor expectations.

Unlike C Corps, LLCs and S Corps are generally not subject to income tax at the entity level. Instead, as in a partnership structure, each of the entity's owners (members of an LLC or stockholders of an S Corp) is allocated its share of the entity's losses and profits, for which it is subject to taxation on a "pass-through basis" that disregards the entity. Entity-level taxation entails "double taxation." A C Corp is taxed on its profits and, if it distributes those profits to its owners via a corporate dividend, the stockholders are also taxed on their income attributable to those funds. "Double taxation" does not sound promising, but the silver lining is that undistributed profits (less entity-level taxes) may accumulate and be reinvested in the business without subjecting the stockholders to liability for individual income tax. By contrast, owners of entities taxed as partnerships are subject to taxation on their share of profits, whether or not they have received a corresponding distribution. Taxation of profits is an important concept—regardless of the harsh reality that most biotechs will not be profitable for many, many years. If the owners have not received a distribution that's equal to their allocable income, they will have received "phantom income." To the extent that the owners' federal, state, and local income tax liability attributable to the phantom income is not matched by commensurate distributions, they will be forced to dip into their own pockets to pay those taxes.

The C Corp has tended to be an almost automatic choice for companies that anticipate seeking venture financing. Historically, venture funds have invested virtually exclusively in C Corps for reasons that include:

- The entity's suitability for a "public exit" via an initial public offering, and venture funds' historical comfort with the C Corp model
- The relatively low transaction costs associated with preparing investment and governance documents for a C Corp
- Contractual arrangements that restrict the receipt by pension plans (and other tax-exempt investors in venture funds) of taxable income from operating companies (which would be allocated to these investors via a fund investment in an LLC)

If venture financing is not in the game plan, an LLC or S Corp is generally the preferable vehicle. Owners, including founders, who are actively involved in the business or able to utilize "passive losses" will be able to offset their share of the entity's losses against other income. However, this can be done only in amounts that do not exceed the amount of the capital they have contributed to the business, plus—in the case of an LLC—certain entity-level debt. If the founders anticipate that the business will become profitable before a sale of the company or another "liquidity event," it usually makes sense to risk the possibility of phantom income in order to take advantage of early losses and save the incremental cost of double taxation. Profitability prior to a liquidity event is a somewhat plausible scenario for diagnostic, tool, or service biotechs—not so much for therapeutics pipelines with long and expensive development paths. Choosing between an LLC and an S Corp is not usually difficult. For most biotech companies (other than for certain consulting and service businesses), the S Corp will not be a viable permanent option, since: (a) federal tax rules bar most non-individual stockholders from investing in an S Corp, and (b) an S Corp is unable to issue preferred stock. Almost all equity investors will demand preferred, rather than common, stock. However, an S Corp has at least one significant advantage over an LLC. All LLC distributions to the founders and other employee owners will be subject to payment of social security (up to the statutory limit) and Medicare taxes. However, an S Corp is generally able to characterize some proportion of its payments to owners as dividends, rather than salary, and *bona fide* dividends will not be subject to these taxes.

It is usually the case that venture funds will not invest shortly after company inception (unless a serial entrepreneur is involved, and/or the entity is a spin-out of a successful parent company). Consequently, the entity anticipates generating losses at the outset. Thus, the choice between a pass-through entity and a C Corp becomes a much closer decision, since owners that are able to utilize the entity's losses will tend to prefer pass-through treatment. This preference will be bolstered by the fact that the transition from an LLC or an S Corp to a C Corp is generally fairly straightforward from both the tax and corporate standpoints (unlike the transition from a C Corp to a pass-through entity, which is generally problematic from a tax perspective). Some advisors warn that forming a pass-through entity signals a potentially damaging tentativeness about the entity's plans to secure venture financing. In our experience, this is generally not the case. Venture funds understand early investors' tax motivations. Moreover, in recent years we have seen an increasing willingness on the part of some venture funds to invest in LLCs. Ultimately, of course, choice of entity, like so many other legal and business decisions, will usually require consideration of multiple factors, including: (a) the projected profit and loss profile of the business over time, (b) proposed financing plans, and (c) the tax preferences of founders and potential investors.

Where should the entity be formed? In most cases, the choice is between Delaware and the home state in which the entity will be based. If the entity is formed in Delaware, certain additional expenses will be incurred. The entity will bear the one-time, incremental cost of formation plus qualification in the home state over the cost of formation in the home state alone (generally several hundred dollars). There are also annual, incremental costs of a similar order of magnitude for maintaining a registered agent in Delaware and paying Delaware franchise taxes (although the Delaware corporate franchise tax can sometimes be considerable). On the plus side, lawyers and investors tend to prefer Delaware. This preference may be less marked for non-corporate entities, if local investors and local counsel are involved, or if the state in question is a major start-up jurisdiction like California or Texas. Of course, factors particular to the individual entity often influence the decision. All things being equal, lawyers generally favor Delaware because its laws and jurisprudence tend to be more up-to-date, sophisticated, extensively developed, and favorable to management (in certain respects) than those of some other jurisdictions. Moreover, Delaware entity law is a nationally-spoken "language" among early-stage investors and attorneys. Delaware is where many biotechs either initially incorporate or eventually re-incorporate—so their laws and procedures are well within an investor's understanding and comfort zone.

THE FOUNDERS AGREEMENT—GET A "PRE-NUP"

Once the founders have reached a decision about the form of organization, the next corporate legal step consists of documenting the understanding between the founders (and any other early investors) that we alluded to at the outset. Principal elements of the understanding may include: the founders' respective roles; the allocation of voting rights and decisional authority; the type of equity that the parties will receive; their respective equity splits and whether each founder's equity will be issued immediately or will be earned in the future; restrictions applicable to the transfer of the equity; and provisions for the company's future growth. It is essential that such principal elements be established as early in the company formation process as possible. Biotechnology is like any other sector, and so is not immune from situations in which the souring of a business relationship potentially diminish or destroy a personal one on the part of the founders. Just as with a marriage, the partners involve do not enter into the relationship anticipating intractable conflict or failure; regardless, it is important to plan for "…the worst of times." Therefore, it is strongly recommended that the founders develop what is the business equivalent of a pre-nuptial agreement ("pre-nup") between those intending to marry. Having a set of pre-determined conditions and provisions cannot stop the dissolution of a business partnership any more than a pre-nup prevents the break-up of a marriage. However, it can decrease the collateral damage and—importantly—lessen the possibility that the company itself is destroyed in the process.

ROLES AND AUTHORITY

Founders need to clearly delineate their respective roles in the company. Each founder brings his or her individual expectations as to equity share, titles, compensation, and decision-making authority. Founders do not necessarily value each other's relative contributions on a consistent or customary basis. They may be short-sighted in attributing value on the basis of temporary circumstances or past contributions, and academic founders, in particular, tend to over-value seniority and tenure. Founders should consider not only their current and near-term standing, which will likely be reflected in the first round of company documentation, but should also be afforded a realistic look at how their position and equity is likely to be affected in the course of the company's development, as new investors come on board. The prospect of "dilution" of the founders' equity position is often a concern; while owners are understandably intent on maintaining their equity percentages to the extent possible, most lawyers have seen deals and companies die because dilutive, but reasonable, transactions were rejected or postponed. Decisions about what each founder is "putting into" and "getting out of" the company should also be consistent with customary start-up arrangements that reflect the expectations of professional investors. Without outside advice, founders may not recognize that their roles will likely change over time, and so their business arrangement must anticipate an evolving situation. Counsel should be on hand to lend these perspectives at an early stage before founders' expectations are set.

Will a particular founder or early investor be active or passive? Will he or she be a director (or in the LLC context, a manager or managing member) of the company or have other decisional rights (*e.g.*, the right to veto or approve specified "major decisions")? Will a majority or a specified supermajority of the owners be needed to approve all decisions (or major decisions)? All or most of the founders may serve as directors (or, in the LLC context, managers or managing members) of the company at the outset; however, these arrangements may or may not survive an initial professional equity round. Investor-appointed directors will be added at that point, but it often makes sense for the company to add "independent," non-founder directors at an earlier time—particularly if the founders are inexperienced, or if there are personality clashes. Founders' roles as employees and consultants to the company will also need to be defined, and appropriate agreements need to be reached regarding compensation, which may build-in equity or other incentives to reward workers (who will likely be foregoing substantial cash rewards at the outset). From the employee's perspective, it is often desirable to have an employment agreement in effect at the earliest possible stage. Having agreement templates may not always be possible (and perhaps not always be desirable from the company standpoint). Nonetheless, employment and compensation arrangements for current executives should be fully formalized no later than the initial venture round.

TYPES OF EQUITY

Founders and early non-professional investors, such as "friends and family," will generally receive common equity. If the company licenses its technology from a university or other research institution, the licensor will also generally receive common equity. Organized angel investors will often, and venture capital firms will virtually always, receive preferred equity. How do these forms of equity differ from one another? In the corporate prototype (which is often "translated" into the LLC context), preferred stock is generally preferred to common stock in three fundamental ways: as to dividends and redemption, as well as upon liquidation. In the start-up context, preferred stock is "convertible" into common stock; as a practical matter, preferred investors rarely elect to convert their preferred prior to an Initial Public Offering (IPO) of stock, or sale of the company. It should also be noted that angel and venture investors often demand and receive other rights, such as voting and decisional rights, tied to their preferred stock, which are beyond the scope of this chapter.

Typically, dividends must be paid to preferred stockholders before they can be paid to common stockholders, and preferred stockholders may have the right to receive a coupon (or cumulative accrual on their investment, akin to interest) prior to the payment of dividends to common stockholders. If and when dividends become payable to common stockholders, preferred stockholders will often "participate" in the common dividends as well. In most biotech contexts, dividends are not paid prior to a sale of the company and therefore dividend rights generally become significant only upon a "liquidation" of the company, as described below. As far as redemption rights are concerned, the company will generally not be permitted to redeem (i.e., repurchase) any shares of common stock before repurchasing the preferred. On the other hand, preferred investors often have a right to "put" their shares of stock to the company and demand their redemption after a specified period of anywhere from 3 to 10 years after their investment.

Finally, and most crucially, preferred stock will be preferred upon liquidation. In this context liquidation refers not only—or even primarily—to the disposition of a failed company's assets, but to any event in which the company's business is effectively sold to outsiders, including a merger or asset sale. The "liquidation preference" is generally equal to the amount of the investment in the preferred stock (or a multiple of that amount) and may also include payment of accrued dividends. Preferred investors will be entitled to their liquidation preference before common stockholders are able to receive any proceeds of the liquidation event; the preferred investors may also (or alternatively) have the right to participate in the liquidation proceeds available to the common stockholders. The purpose of the liquidation preference is to ensure that the preferred stockholders recoup their investment, plus a specified return, prior to the receipt by common stockholders of any acquisition proceeds. Preferred stockholders are therefore "covered" if the company achieves sufficient success to be sold, but not enough to achieve a return for all stockholders; if a company does not achieve a sufficient return, venture investors may take all the acquisition proceeds.

Generally, preferred equity is issued in multiple series, each of which has somewhat different rights. Common equity may also be of different types, of which non-voting common is perhaps the most prevalent type.

EQUITY SPLITS AND EQUITY PLANS

The equity share that founders and other early participants in the venture receive is considered as part of the founders' deliberative process. As indicated, the process involves an implied valuation of each participant's contributions relative to the others. By extension, it also involves a more or less explicit relative valuation of the intellectual property and other assets being acquired by the entity, the cash being contributed, and the value of the founders' efforts (to the extent not covered by promised compensation). Because the bulk of these efforts will likely be exerted in the future, the company has an interest in incentivizing employees (as well as directors and consultants), and therefore some portion of their equity will be subject to future issuance, usually following the grant and exercise of options. Shares of stock may also be issued on a current basis, in the form of restricted stock that is subject to divestment or repurchase by the company. In the LLC context, equity incentives generally take the form of profits interests which, as the term implies, consist of a percentage interest in the entity's profits—but does not include a share of the entity's capital.

Typically, a start-up will reserve anywhere from 10 to 20% of its fully-diluted equity for management equity plans or "pools." The split of equity among different executive and other positions will often follow customary guidelines. Equity will generally vest over a period of three to five years. If equity plans are not in place at the time of the initial venture round, venture funds will typically require that the arrangements be formalized at that time. Founding corporate documents should include a legal mechanism to increase the pool for subsequent offerings to employees, advisors, board members, etc. There should be a balance between the extent to which the option pool can be expanded and the number/percentage of available options. This information is part of a company's "capitalization table" (or "cap table") and is very important to prospective investors, since it quickly and concisely shows who owns the company and how much each person owns.

The tax rules governing equity compensation are complex, and each of the commonly-employed equity compensation vehicles has its own pitfalls. Common (and costly) errors from a tax standpoint include the failure of an employee or consultant stockholder to make a timely "Section 83(b) election," as well as the issuance by the start-up of options at below-market rates (including the failure to properly document the value of the stock). In the former situation, had the election been timely made, the stock would have been taxable as compensation to the recipient based upon the relatively low (and perhaps nominal) value of the stock at the time of receipt. If, instead, the election is not timely made, the tax is triggered on the presumably much-greater value of the stock when the restriction lapses, despite the fact that the stockholder will not necessarily have any liquidity at that time which would enable the stockholder to pay the tax. In the latter situation, running afoul of Section 409A of the Internal Revenue Code may subject the option holder to prohibitive taxes, interest, and penalties.

RESTRICTIONS ON TRANSFER

The founders will usually want to restrict transferability of the company's equity. There are several common motives for these restrictions: (1) the founders have agreed to be "partners," but they have not consented to the admission of unknown others; (2) unloading equity represents a diminished commitment on the part of the selling owner, including potentially diminished efforts on the company's behalf; and (3) the company will want to restrict offers and sales of equity that may run afoul of federal or state securities laws. Restrictions on transfer often take the form of a "blanket" prohibition, followed by limited exceptions for "permitted transfers" (often including transfers for estate-planning purposes or transfers by a corporate owner to related individuals or entities), and by provisions that subject "non-permitted transfers" to rights of first refusal and tag-along rights. Rights of first refusal generally require a prospective seller of company equity to afford the company and/or the other owners the opportunity to match the price a third party may be willing to pay to the prospective seller, enabling the company or insiders to trump the proposed sale to the third party and keep the equity "within the family." Tag-along rights (also known as participation or come-along rights) will come into play only if the rights of first refusal are not exercised. In that case, the tag-along affords the other stockholders the right to participate in the third-party sale, so that one owner does not benefit from a favorable rush to the exit ahead of the other owners. Both sets of rights will generally be exercised by owners on a *pro rata* basis (i.e., in proportion to their percentage ownership) and, after a professional funding round, may be confined to the preferred investors. In any event, the very existence of these rights will make it quite difficult for a prospective seller to find a buyer, quite apart from the fact that the sale of illiquid private company equity is often a difficult proposition. As a result, these rights generally come into play very infrequently. The provisions should certainly be properly drafted, but founders (and some lawyers) sometimes get too caught up in some of the attendant contingencies.

PROVISIONS FOR FUTURE GROWTH

Provisions for future growth include empowering the board (in a corporate context) to issue preferred stock without stockholder approval and (in both the corporate and LLC contexts) enabling amendments of the founders agreement by consent of a specified majority, rather than requiring unanimity. Along similar lines, "drag-along" provisions require all owners to approve and sell their equity in a company sale event if the sale is approved by a specified majority of the owners, and conversion provisions enable LLCs to be "converted" into other corporate forms, usually in order to meet investor requirements. Preemptive rights provisions enable existing owners to buy into new investment rounds and maintain their relative percentage ownership of the company. Other provisions of this general type include registration rights, which enable stockholders to sell their shares of stock in a public offering. After a professional funding round, many of these rights may be re-engineered and confined to the preferred investors, or the preferred investors may receive priority treatment.

FORM OF FOUNDERS AGREEMENT; COMMON MISTAKES

The founders' understanding will typically be documented in a corporate stockholders agreement (and may also be reflected in the corporate charter and by-laws), or an LLC operating agreement. Corporate divisions of authority among stockholders (who generally have statutory or contractual authority over a limited number of major decisions), directors (who have full managerial authority with respect to matters outside the ordinary course of business, subject to the rights of stockholders), and officers (whose authority extends only to day-to-day matters and implementing board decisions) are more clearly defined than the corresponding divisions of authority in the LLC context, where the operating agreement will generally define the authority of members on one hand, and that of any managers or officers, on the other. In practice, the "division of authority" in the start-up LLC context tends to follow the corporate start-up model. Both the LLC and corporation (to a somewhat lesser degree) offer considerable flexibility and room for individual variation on the start-up theme; however, founders should resist the impulse to craft overly creative, complex, or idiosyncratic arrangements. Departing from customary templates tends to be more costly to document, and it may alienate prospective investors.

Complex arrangements sometimes arise during the negotiation of founder arrangements—particularly in situations where individual counsel is retained by some or all of the founders. While the retention of individual counsel is sometimes necessary and beneficial to individual founders (and even, ultimately, to the venture), in our experience, founders should generally make every effort to be jointly represented. Not only will the retention of separate counsel be more expensive and potentially counterproductive in terms of the deal/documentary result, it also tends to magnify differences between the founders, impairs team spirit, and may alert outsiders to a fatal lack of company solidarity

Founders should also bear in mind that their arrangements will likely undergo considerable revision once professional investors come on board. Founders will need to deal with issues relevant to the pre-professional investment period. They may wish to "position" certain elements of their deal in anticipation of an investment round. Still, they generally do not need to deal with contingencies like a sale of the company or an IPO, which can only arise after (usually, considerably after) the initial professional rounds of investment.

More common than overly elaborate founder arrangements is the tendency to err in the opposite direction by failing to adequately specify the necessary elements of the deal, or to document them in a binding and complete manner. Worse still, the company may commit to a deal that does not "work" from a business or legal standpoint. Apart from items already mentioned, the unsavory list of common start-up mistakes includes:

- Issuing equity without a clear exemption from applicable securities laws
- Granting unusual anti-dilution rights to investors
- Contracting with spurious "finders"
- Failing to properly secure rights to intellectual property produced by employees and consultants
- Failing to pay employees or employment taxes
- Treating personnel that meet the legal criteria for employment as independent contractors
- Failing to properly implement or observe confidentiality restrictions (business realities can be dramatically different from academic norms in this area)
- Failing to properly "diligence" or investigate counterparties and transactions
- Failing to obtain necessary insurance coverage

This depressing list could be extended indefinitely, but we prefer to return to an earlier theme. You need not repeat these mistakes. The right lawyers are out there, waiting and willing to help and partner with you. Really.

CHAPTER 3

Building Your Team

Henry Miller
SVP & Global Practice Head, SPG Life Sciences Executive Search

L ife science entrepreneurs, whether they are experienced or simply starting out the first time, are continuously challenged by myriad pressures and challenges. There are funding challenges, meetings with (actual and potential) investors, site selection, science considerations, and other areas to factor daily. A foundational element to business creation and success is surrounding oneself with a solid team. These initial key hires are the ones that allow for hurtling out of the starting blocks and beginning the race that will help all move ahead. An entrepreneur is often looking for the "one way to do this" or the "best way." The reality is that different situations allow for different solutions—and no one way of building or hiring your team will apply to every solution. What is available is a series of steps and actionable plans that will assist the executive in making a series of rational and intelligent decisions. From a career in helping senior executives make quality hiring decisions, the reader will learn real life examples that should aid in helping start strong and finish well in forming a solid life science team. These insights into real success and failure are rarely revealed beyond the doors of search firms and venture capital (VC) offices. Opening these doors wide, the reader will be informed of potential success angles. The areas covered are as follows:

- Assumptions
- All Aboard
- Channels for Hiring
- Be Aware

As the reader starts down the entrepreneurial path in a life science organization, be assured of several facts that have proven near universally true in other biotechnology professionals careers and experience:

- Funding is always needed
- Timelines will be shortened and results expectation increased, at the same time, always
- Biotechnology teams will do more hands-on work personally than ever before
- Many of your network who were thought to support the decision to go biotech, will not
- "Marketing responsibility," regardless of title, is a must
- Being a leader with real ability to impact results is its own reward
- Regardless of outcome, rejoining "Big Pharma" or tenured academia will be difficult

Nearly every CEO in a biotechnology or life science start-up is always on the lookout for funding or future partners, while concurrently concerned about cash burn and cash flow. If joining from Big Pharma, simply get used to this reality. Fortunately, some of the best funding partnerships are available from those same organizations you may have recently left. In the world of VC and private equity, partnerships, and even angel investing, the need to demonstrate results and understand return on investment (ROI)—constantly and consistently—is paramount. This is not an environment for the faint of heart—and hiring people that understand this element is vital to managing expectations and emerging with worthy results.

Big Pharma hires are splashy—but are they wise? If your team is solely assembled with emigrants from Big Pharma, be forewarned that much of the day-to-day effort formerly passed on to staff may now fall to senior management or departmental managers alone. Staff is minimal. Delegation to outsourced partners like contract research organizations (CROs) is possible, but the staggering reality is that you will not be able to avoid activities that you may not have personally done in years, or ever. In addition, the cost of "virtual" assistance—while usually lower than a full-time employee—can still be substantial. Before you hire, determine whether your candidate is ready to pull together themselves the clinical trial data, evaluate clinical data management applications, conduct site visits, and evaluate and hold accountable various vendors. In the end, your team will also likely be presenting everything you are doing—relating to expenditures and results—to your investors and board of directors. This is a huge consideration for hiring and deciding cultural fit. We will touch on ways to evaluate potential success before the offer is extended.

We all need support. However, believing that certain current loyal employees or colleagues will join you, or that others will invest in your venture, is a short-lived reality once the organization begins. Remember this venture is a new entity, with a yet to be defined culture. And many who you have interacted with in the past will encourage you, but will want no personal part in the operation. Rely on promises faintly, if at all. As an entrepreneur, remember that if it is not in writing, it is not real. Do not assume anything in this area, as it can stop businesses before they really even start.

In many large pharma organizations the "science" of the business is separated from the "commercial" or marketing side. I have met many a chief scientific officer or head of discovery that consider marketing and selling to be not in their area of responsibilities. Welcome to start-up land where everyone is expected to contribute to the marketing of the future of the organization. All of the start-up executives will become familiar with the "road show" if an initial public offering is in your future. On a weekly basis, each executive will be internally and externally properly positioning and "selling" the company.

For first-time entrepreneurs, understand that mistakes are unavoidable and 99% of the time recoverable. The good news is that you and the executive team are those most responsible for business success—and that is also the challenge. Everything comes back to you in rewards and errors. Building an organization is a joy to most executives and results are obvious for your efforts, whereas your impact in a larger organization may be more difficult to assess, regardless of your title or role. In other words, there is nowhere to hide, and that should be seen as a positive for the right-minded life science start-up executive.

Lastly, evidence indicates that most executives who enjoy the start-up organization find it very difficult to return to large or midsize pharma or academia. The operational and intrinsic rewards are very significant regardless of the eventual level of success. If your start-up organization is eventually acquired or commercializes its product, the financial reward will likely outweigh what others have spent careers to earn in large pharma organizations. An informal poll of executives in transition indicates that nearly all are seeking a small-to-midsize company if they have recently left one of those similar organizations. They feel buried in the corporate organization charts of a larger company. Perspectives have changed.

That's the great news. Whenever we put ourselves in a position to take on a new challenge in our employment, we grow in some way. That change will stay with us for the remainder of our careers and, for the most part, is a positive.

ASSUMPTIONS

All of us carry assumptions. These are based on belief, fact, conjecture, or others' opinion. When building your team, it is fine to rely on experience. However, minimizing your assumptions is strongly encouraged in order to grow effectively. With first-time entrepreneurs, consideration of what your team should "look like" often centers on the following three questions:

- With whom have I previously worked?
- Who do my investors say we need to hire?
- Who is affordable and/or available?

In my years as a senior level executive recruiter, I have observed many an executive consider the first bullet above as their initial inclination for team building. If you, as CEO or founder, are coming from Big Pharma, you may think that Dr. Smith (your pharma colleague) would be a wonderful addition to your executive team. It is a natural thought, given your years of working together. However, it is a dangerous assumption in many ways. While you have likely embraced the small company entrepreneurial environment, Dr. Smith may have given it little thought or no thought at all. Has he/she been in larger pharmaceutical companies his entire career? Does he/she currently rely completely on a full and devoted staff for the heavy lifting that could quickly become a daily grind for the unprepared executive?

A major assumption new biotechnology executives make is that "others" share their passion. Without the Big Pharma names of Pfizer, BMS, Merck, etc., to back up who you are and what you do, many senior biotechnology executives have a withdrawal and adjustment period that must be minimized, as time is paramount for your investors and the company. One CEO I have worked with in a start-up biotechnology company was from a large pharma organization in the U.S. midwest. This newly-minted CEO was completely transfixed on hiring two key players from his past company. He mistook their enthusiasm for his move as an endorsement of his company plan and vision. Further clouding his awareness of their eventual reluctance to relocate to the new company on the east coast was his personal friendship with these professionals. The reality check came in two parts. Initially, they came and interviewed and were intrigued. In hindsight, my assessment was that they were curious rather than interested. As an entrepreneur, you will need to throw out your assumptions and approach each hire—especially those you "know"—with a scientific approach to gauge their true interest. This CEO felt his former colleagues would love to join—but never really asked them outright the challenging questions. Core questions need to be asked of all potential candidates, such as:

- Now that you have been brought up to speed, tell me:

what interests you most?
- How does your spouse feel about the relocation?
- Are school choice or educational decisions part of your evaluation?
- Could you see yourself working in [*this city*]?
- Can your home be sold (what is your equity situation)?

Regardless of the former colleague's skill, they need to want to be in the new organization. They need to state why they want to be a part of it clearly and with no hesitation. If they are just coming along for interviews to "kick the tires," you will spend time, money and goodwill with your partners and investors chasing something that ultimately has a very low probability of happening. Just because you worked with great people in your prior organization, there is virtually no basis that they will eventually join you. The university or company you left may do an all out press to retain them, including promotion. You need to ask them why they are interested and evaluate the answer.

For the entrepreneur, it is standard practice to set up shop within a reasonable commute of here they live. Consequently, relocation for the entrepreneur coming from academia or a medical research center may seem a moot point. Relocation for the entrepreneur leaving a company for their own start-up may seem a moot point as well. Lastly, it is unnecessary and somewhat preposterous for the entrepreneur in-licensing technology from a company or university to move to where the licensor is located. So, why and when does relocation eventually become a factor? Because most—not all, but most—biotechnology companies, will require equity investment at some point. Typically, this means VC. And the rumor that VCs like to be near their money is true. VCs will want to keep an eye on their investment—even if only four times per year at quarterly board of directors meetings. They could want you to move your operations to where most financiers are located: Boston and San Francisco being the two major centers. It is also easier for them to build your team—especially with seasoned, successful business acumen—if your company is located where money and talent are more readily in supply.

Therefore, relocation is not something an entrepreneur needs worry about right away—yet it should be part of the general list of issues he/she may need to one day face.

Spousal or partner considerations are paramount these days, as are having school-age children. In past years, the "company people" took the relocation and made the move. This is far less true today. I spoke recently with a chief commercial officer who moved nine times in 20 years, and swore to her family they would not relocate. With headquarters for her new company moving, her choice was to take an apartment in the new city and have her teenage children and husband will stay in their current home and not relocate. With less than 5 years to work before her planned retirement, this may work for her, but it is difficult and generally not recommended for a start-up. Spouses are full partners, and our experience as search professionals reflects that if relocation stresses a relationship, the company will lose. They lose immediately in terms of productivity and engagement and often in the end they also actually lose the employee, who wants to keep their personal relationship intact.

Education for children is a delicate matter that most human resource professionals recognize as near paramount in relocations. One of the real dangers of being an executive is looking at the world through your own prism. You have likely gone through a series of decisions, evaluations, and discussions to arrive at the point where you were ready to take on this leader or co-leader in a biotechnology role. As you assemble a team, your timing as a start-up company will generally not allow these potential employees to go through the same full process. You need to build your team quickly. We live in an age where some children test into grade school and begin SAT training early as well. Many kids have private coaches/clinics for athletics and hobbies. Children today have much more say in the process of relocation, either directly or due to a parents concern. There was a time when children and spouses went with the breadwinner, but that can no longer be assumed. Disruption is the buzzword I hear often when making recruiting calls. Generally, grade-school children are easiest to blend into a move. However, parents are very reluctant in middle school and teenage years to voluntary relocate short of financial hardship needs. Our firm has internal metrics that reflect that if a job involves relocation out of state, nearly 65% of professional life science people would not consider, *unless* it was a accompanied by a significant improvement in responsibility, authority, and financial reward. Although your start-up will likely offer some of the above, you usually cannot fairly insert the word "significant." As an extreme example, a large pharmaceutical client of ours has an up-and-coming group of executives in Europe for whom they would like a U.S. rotation for 2 years. As an inducement, the company has paid for a language tutor, to be based in the U.S., for their children in their native tongue. This inducement was employed so these young children would not fall behind on proficiency once they return home. So, relocation challenges are a global phenomenon. While you will not likely follow to the above example to induce an executive, it shows what expectations your team will face in the recruitment effort.

The location also needs to be sold. One of the major concerns heard in biotechnology start-ups is that they are not in major biopharma corridors. The major biotechnology hubs in New England and San Francisco, and the major pharmaceutical corridor in New Jersey through Pennsylvania, are among the strongest areas to place a business because of the proximity of partners, investors, and talent. The mid-Atlantic, Research Triangle of North Carolina, and Pacific Northwest are not as vibrant, but continue to make substantial progress. Often, executive search and human resources (HR) professionals will hear that candidates are concerned that they will be away from their professional network if a job does not work out in a remote city. These concerns are real, and definitely inhibit successfully attracting and on boarding talent.

Lastly, and importantly, are financial issues of relocation. While most start-ups are in no position to purchase a home for a coveted executive candidate, offering a relocation package is often required. At minimum, these packages generally cover movement of household goods. Most professionals in relocation have seen a sizeable number of collapsed moves based on low equity and being underwater in home ownership during economic downturns—such as the one that began in 2007. At such times, real estate appreciation stops, and those that may have bought in past 3-5 years may not have the equity to sell their home with enough money for a another down-payment. Economic down-turns affect both major companies and start-ups, severely limiting relocation potential.

While the above points do not address every assumption or challenge you will face, it does get to the core group of issues we have seen as service professionals relating to the ability to attract people. Next, we will examine the positions you need, and when it is best to consider bringing such expertise on board.

ALL ABOARD

There are differing opinions about the timing of certain hires in the biotechnology space. You will undoubtedly need a chief executive officer (CEO—or chief operations officer [COO] if you intend to fill this role for the time being), business development leader, chief scientific officer (CSO), and chief medical officer (CMO). A recent must-have is a head of commercial. Funding is traditionally a driver of many of the roles; while that is important, one must generally think ahead in order to prioritize planning for success.

The CEO is most often in place with funding, or he/she forms the company to seek funding. This person is generally a medical or scientific professional who has already morphed into a general management executive over the course of their career. If the founding CEO is more scientifically-comfortable than business-savvy, expect that investors will want a funding-focused CEO at some point. Investors will make their return following a "liquidity event"—the sale, acquisition, or initial public offering (IPO) of an organization—and the science oriented professional will carry the title of co-founder but be placed where they can add the most value. It is important to understand that while investors and the company executives both want to see success, their definition of success may differ. A medical professional may want to see a disease eliminated, while a group of investors with board representation may see an early stage offer from Big Pharma as a goal, either in partnership or buyout form. Regardless, the CEO—in whatever form—will be one of the initial roles in the company.

A vice president of business development, or similarly titled professional, is extremely important early on. They can forge effective partnerships with other companies on licensing, or other areas that can assist in creating revenue streams without diluting equity to the current investors and management. Beyond this, they can and should be an invaluable part of the team that creatively shapes the financial health of the business and creates planning options by virtue of the relationships they build.

A CSO will be needed at the beginning from all fronts science-related. They will work closely with research partners and internal discovery and preclinical efforts, as well as potential third parties. They will have an immense level of responsibility to be technically sound, as well as have a business orientation to direct efforts toward success. They are the thought-leader representative. Ideally, they should be passionate personable advocates of your company. Shy, or ivory-tower types, will prove much less effective.

CMOs and chief commercial officers are sometimes not brought in until some major achievements have been made that lean toward commercialization. We often see a biotechnology that has a CEO with an MD degree, so the need for a separate CMO is not initially paramount. However, many biotechnology companies are now bringing in teams of professionals very early; long before the first product in the pipeline is on the cusp of commercialization. Commercial heads are joining early because investors want to make sure that the sometimes overly-scientific founding team is shaping the organization into something that will be acquired—or at least seem attractive to a partner.

In all of the above areas, it is likely investor groups will want input on building the team. Their investment may also have conditions on board of directors representation and input. While not inherently wrong or uncommon, as a hiring executive you need to fully understand that the success or failure of the organization will be your responsibility. Therefore, simply hiring who your investors and advisors tell you is best is not good leadership.

On the other hand, many investors are well-versed on the challenges in beginning a high functioning organization out of the starting gate, and can offer excellent advice and perspective on the types of people you need, and even who may be a best fit. However, your team should ultimately be your choice, as you are the one who will need to live with the decision. There are wonderful examples of cooperation and collaboration in hiring executives with input from their advisors and investors—as well as potential negative outcomes. One major caveat is that, if you are the top executive, and hiring another C-level team member is recommended by investors/board members, make sure the new executive reports to you. No news should go to their outside colleagues or "other friends" without your awareness. The team members' allegiances must be to each other for the success of the organization.

It is appropriate to mention why hiring a "big name" executive may not be a wise move. Recall that hiring is about skill assessment first—then cultural fit. Sometimes a great candidate is presented that has both in abundance. However, this executive may be accustomed to the accolades and attention that go along with being a key opinion leader. Perhaps that executive is a highly recognized renowned MD who will be heading your medical effort, and will be a point person in your communication efforts. Ultimately, they need to understand and accept their supportive—albeit critical—role.

No matter who and what positions come on at the early stage of a biotechnology organization, it is safe to assume that a deadline-focused, results-oriented communication style is imperative. Investor groups, medical partners, and even patient advocacy groups (*e.g.*, foundations, another potential funding source) will be interested in your success and setbacks. Inevitably, there will be both. Several executives will be "point people" who will communicate with the media, board, and key outsiders (referral sources, investors, etc.). It is vital to have an honest, ongoing, factual process to ensure that no unintentional inconsistencies come up in the dialogue with others. The message must be clear and the result of consensus.

As a rule of thumb, very early-stage companies may have a team comprised of a president/CEO (often a founder), technical/research/clinical leader (there are various titles applicable here, including CSO, and CMO) and someone to assist with partnering or business development. The business development leader is a more urgent priority in order to create revenue opportunities for the near- and long-term health of the enterprise. As the organization matures, additional funding options may present themselves. Staff will be brought as needed to deal with the operational needs at that time.

It is not uncommon today to hear of "virtual" biotechnology companies. Although formerly limited to start-ups, it is now seen by many companies as a long-term strategic path. These are full biotechnology organizations intentionally limiting their business footprint to a small number of full-time employees (FTEs). They "outsource" (i.e., bring on from outside the organization) everything beyond core science and business needs. They draw upon consultants or service providers to outsource human resources, clinical operations, finance, and other areas until they believe that they need that group in-house or never. Many self-described virtual businesses expect to eventually sell the organization and its intellectual capital to a larger company, and will not add staff in many areas. This models a trend in major pharmaceutical organizations of outsourcing non-core services, and is one that the reader should be aware of—and consider— in constructing their organization.

CHANNELS FOR HIRING

The core methods for attracting a team to the emerging biotechnology organization are:

- Personal network (current and former colleagues/ advisors)
- Advertising (broadly)
- Third party recruitment

We have already covered recommendations from investors or boards; the above three are standard manners in which to identify and attract talent. Each has advantages and drawbacks which will need to be weighed.

A personal network is limited by nature of your contacts. However, the inherent trust and knowledge of the group is a positive in many ways. One of the challenges of using your professional network is the amount of time you will be personally using to identify and evaluate the best and interested parties. Many entrepreneurs are frustrated to find that the best are sometimes just not interested. A significant limitation is that one's personal network, while potentially wide, is generally narrower than needed to truly identify the widest group of talent. Tapping personal networks is generally cost-effective, in that no money is exchanged for working this avenue.

Online and print advertising can range from zero to several thousand dollars. Help wanted ads for executives are mostly a thing of the past in the United States; online ads are used for the majority of advertising. Online ads have the advantage of reaching a broad audience, and can be crafted in a more targeted manner. Note that keeping the company and targeted therapeutic under the radar will not be possible; too little information in an ad will not generate interest. The biggest drawback with advertising is that it actually generates a massive response from poorly qualified professionals that may need to be heavily managed in terms of expectations. Be prepared for an onslaught of email and mailed resumes to arrive. One consideration to have is that these "applicants" often expect feedback or a response and generally that is not a reasonable possibility for the company hiring. If these applicants are in your general area of therapeutic focus, this could cause a backlash later down the road.

Third-party recruitment generally takes the two forms. Both involving a fee for service.

A retained search firm is generally paid an up-front fee to "search" for the best talent based on your must have criteria. Expect to have some mapping of the candidates and a strong short list of candidates who are interested and readily available with notice. These candidates will generally not have been searching for a new position, and have been recruited on your behalf by the search firm. Up-front fees are required, and access to the best talent should be expected. The retained executive search professional should have experience with your need and clearly outline deliverables in advance. Guarantee periods are generally 6 months to 1 year for the placed executive.

Contingency firms are generally paid a fee upon hire of candidate. This creates an incentive to the contingency recruiter to get the job done quickly. By nature of their business model, many of these organizations will not perform search mapping, but rather rely on a large database of "quasi-active candidates" with whom they may have a past connection. A guarantee on placement of 90 days maximum should be expected with a contingency firm.

All models of recruitment have their place and rationale in a biotechnology start-up, and your team will need to decide on the best approach through evaluation of the level of talent needed, coupled with the timeline available for each hire.

BE AWARE

In the book "Good to Great," Jim Collins discusses the overall need to "get the right people on the bus." While this relates to having the right people pulling together and is vitally important, the start-up executive needs to understand that the bus route may change. Your organization could be focused on a specific disease area, and subsequent clinical studies could indicate that a different disease area has more potential for your organization. The successful entrepreneur will be cautious to bring on board people who can be broad enough to accomplish tasks when the road to success unintentionally alters.

Secondly, cultures will change as the organization develops. Should the organization grow successfully from discovery through clinical and toward commercial, it would not be uncommon to see several changes in senior management along the way. The executives who are needed at one stage may be swapped out for philosophical reasons, ability to scale with growth, burnout, or a myriad of other reasons. As an entrepreneur, do not be caught in the trap of seeking perfect candidates for initial appointment. Finding the "perfect team" for the life of the organization is not realistic. Find the team that can help now and into a reasonable future of approximately 3-5 years. If you are fixated on the candidates who are "perfect" in all ways, you will have a difficult time leading forward with growth. Expect change and hire the best available, but be aware of cultural fit and reality of time expectations as much as required skill to accomplish the task.

One of the common hiring models is bringing on board major pharmaceutical employees into biotechnology companies. As discussed earlier, it is critical to be aware that many underestimate the required pace and effort needed to create success. Often, a mid-level executive with potential will have an opportunity to take on a more senior role in a biotechnology company. This can be a safer hire at times based on their likelihood to having recently performed a lot of the day to day duties that a VP from Big Pharma may no longer be familiar with. In other words, they can be incredible workhorses and committed to proving their value. Unfortunately, as the company grows, they may not be able to manage the levels of employees and breadth that may come to pass. Again, be aware that you are building the team for today into tomorrow and that changes are likely.

In terms of general qualities and experiences sought in a biotechnology executive (beyond the required technical acumen), experience reflects that a "wish list" would include the following:

- Experience in Big Pharma and biotechnology organizations
- Drive for results
- Ability to influence without authority
- Ambitious
- Team oriented
- Politically astute
- Managerial experience
- Commercially aware

Experience in Big Pharma, as well as a prior biotechnology role, suggests a very solid set of experiences. The rationale is that the candidate understands what works well in major pharmaceutical and also equally what parts are dysfunctional and should be left at the door upon joining. If the candidate also has smaller company experience, it is seen as good preparation for the rigor and pace (and potential lack of resources) in a biotechnology organization. Having experiences in both minimizes the strains of the job, and allows one to pull other team members on the journey toward success.

A drive for results is generally sought in all candidates for most jobs. However, the biotechnology executive needs to have a deep reservoir of self-motivation and drive, given constraints of time and resources while working in a regulated environment with investors and boards seeking results in a timely fashion. When interviewing prospective candidates, it is important to seek examples of explicit above and beyond results while under pressure.

Influencing without authority is vital in a smaller company, and can be a great asset in a large organization. In a biotechnology start-up, there will be colleagues and vendors that you will need to influence to aid you in keeping your process moving ahead. In a larger organization, you may be able to pull rank as a VP and people may treat you with deference. This works far less effectively in a smaller company where everyone is overworked and pushing hard.

Ambition may take several forms. Ambition for the science to save lives and treat disease is one type. Personal ambition for success is another. Both are optimal to some degree in being a part of a start-up. What must be avoided is a blind ambition to climb to the next title and triumph against all odds. Such a mind-set is completely at odds with the important concept of the "team." Team orientation is a must. The biotechnology professional will be a part of a small co-dependent group in the success of this endeavor. Proper teamwork and subjugation of egos to the benefit of the research and discovery is a must. Those that do not exhibit team orientation are often quickly relieved of duty.

Being politically astute is a beneficial skill as it allows one to see through agendas and personal schemes that may inhibit company success. It is especially important for executives as they will need to read into partnerships and collaborations. Being politically astute is very different from being a political person. The latter can do great damage in the culture of a smaller company. It puts a person's attention of and effort on what is best for them individually. However, being astute allows those in charge to keep their focus on nurturing productive aspirations in their team

Managerial experience is a prerequisite for any role in a biotechnology organization that involves managing people. Generally, these organizations are moving so quickly that having the time to teach management of other people is not possible. Most executives cite bad management as one of the top reasons why people leave an organization. The biotech can generally ill-survive rapid turnover—so bringing someone into the organization without successful managerial expertise is generally risky.

Commercially-aware professionals are wanted in a biotechnology organization. Traditionally non-business/commercial executives—from the medical doctors to the scientists—need to be aware that to have a company success, a market must exist that is willing to pay. Some larger company scientific leaders may consider themselves above the commercial needs, exhibiting an attitude that science and commercialism cannot co-exist. A biotechnology manager and leader must find a way to have them work together for a greater good.

SUMMARY

If you are considering a role at a biotechnology organization, consider whether you truly have the energy and enthusiasm to work in a pressured environment on a daily basis. If you are adding talent to your existing organization, use some of the above as criteria, but also find the important ingredients for success unique to your organization and hire against those with stated and written criteria.

One very important element left out of the above discussion is to speak deeply and in detail to professionals who have gone before you in the world of biotechnology. Seek out their triumphs and setbacks, and learn from them as you build your team. Communication and networking are as essential as solid science backed up with effective clinical trials. Some of the greatest medical discoveries have arisen from biotechnology efforts. Joining the industry and driving ahead for results can be a rewarding experience for life.

Congratulations on the decision.

CHAPTER 4

Intellectual Property Protection and Strategy

Nancy W. Vensko, JD*
Partner, Fitch, Even, Tabin & Flannery

INTRODUCTION: GETTING A PATENT

Intellectual property (IP) is defined as a property right protecting products of the human intellect, constituting mainly trademarks, copyrights, and patents, but also trade secrets. Commercializing new drugs and laboratory tests often depends on the existence of patent protection. Typically, small companies in-license technologies from universities and research institutes or develop technologies in-house, with the goal to out-license technologies or partner with large companies.

What are some points to consider in the decision to get a patent? Under what my colleague, Thomas F. Lebens, calls the "patent business triangle," the invention must be patentable, a market needs to exist, and you have to be able to meet the demand. This chapter will focus on the "invention" side of the triangle.

---

* Disclaimer: The information and material in this chapter are provided for informational purposes only. This chapter does not provide legal advice. This chapter does not necessarily reflect the opinions of Fitch, Even, Tabin & Flannery (FETF) or Sinsheimer Juhnke Lebens & McIvor (SJLM) or their clients. Reading this chapter and/or contacting FETF or SJLM based on this chapter does not create an attorney-client relationship between you and FETF or SJLM.

Kenneth W. Dam, as well as other economists, describes the economics underlying patents.[1] These government grants reward research and development (R&D) in exchange for a "limited right" to exclude others from copying the patented invention during the term of the patent. If companies could not recover the costs of R&D because the invention could be copied by all, then we could expect a much lower level of innovation. Patents fix the copying problem so that a company can recover the costs of R&D. This is how patents stimulate innovation and incentivize new drugs and laboratory tests.

Biotechnology is an industry having a business model that is based on taking significant risks to develop new drugs. Specifically, the biotechnology business model is based on R&D of new chemicals, such as proteins and genes, which become new drugs. Joseph A. DiMasi and colleagues report that the average cost of bringing a new drug from concept all the way to FDA approval is about $800 million and that it takes about 10 years.[2]

Take, for example, the case of thyroid-stimulating hormone (TSH) of US patent no. 6,284,491. Many valuable proteins occur in nature only in minute quantities, or are difficult to purify from natural sources. The availability of substantially pure TSH made the diagnosis and treatment of human thyroid cancer a reality. Previously, the only available method to diagnose and treat human thyroid cancer involved administering cadaver-originating TSH to stimulate the uptake of radioactive iodine into the cancer. All of the diagnostic tests and treatments depended upon high levels of human TSH. However, there was not enough natural product available from human pituitaries collected at autopsies. Furthermore, even if available, the human pituitaries had been found to be contaminated with viruses. As a result, the regulatory authorities had forbidden the use of the natural product for any human diagnostic or treatment studies.

The diagnosis and treatment of thyroid cancer now involves cloning the gene for TSH and using it to make "recombinant" TSH. Recombinant TSH means making TSH by cloning the gene. TSH is now available in large quantities and is uncontaminated with viruses or other by-products of collecting human pituitaries from autopsies.

Although the exact cost of bringing this new drug from concept to FDA approval has not been disclosed, a figure anywhere near the DiMasi estimated average would represent a significant investment. By virtue of a "limited right," patents let companies recoup the high cost of R&D, thus giving companies an incentive to invest in new drugs and laboratory tests.

Yet, on the reasoning that the price for obtaining a single US patent is about $25,000 to $50,000, if you want a 10-fold return on investment then the technology needs to net $250,000 to $500,000 over the lifetime of the patent. Perhaps the invention can easily be protected as a trade secret, making patenting unnecessary; a trade secret is information that derives independent economic value from not being generally known or readily ascertainable by others, and is the subject of reasonable efforts to maintain its secrecy. Should the invention not easily be protected as a trade secret, then you need to balance the benefits of getting a patent against the costs.

If the patent covers an invention that has hefty R&D costs, getting a patent may be worthwhile. Recall that the economics underlying patents hold that patents on an invention having hefty R&D costs prevent competitors (*e.g.*, those that have no R&D costs) from undercutting the price, and thus permit the innovator to recover the costs of invention. Even a patent on an invention that does not have hefty R&D costs may be profitable by reason of increasing prices, restricting use, and securing investment.[3]

Additionally, if the patent covers an "improvement," which, although patentable, infringes a prior unexpired patent for a "pioneering" invention, the cost-benefit analysis may favor getting a patent. This is because the owner of the prior unexpired patent would need a license to make, use, or sell your improvement. While you, yourself, would need to license the prior unexpired patent to make, use, or sell your own improvement, cross-licensing could save you both from infringement liability.

Patenting an improvement which, although patentable, infringes a patent for a "pioneering" invention, does not grant you a freedom-to-operate. You should probably seek a right-to-use search, also called a freedom-to-operate search, before you manufacture, use, or sell an allegedly patented thing. As you will see, a patent grants you a right to exclude others from trespassing on your intellectual property, but not a right to trespass on the intellectual property of others.

This chapter will examine the basics about patents, formal requirements for getting a patent, substantive conditions for getting a patent, the meaning of a "statutory bar," the meaning of a "printed publication," suggestions for preparing an invention disclosure describing a discovery sought to be patented for technologies you develop in-house, the fundamentals about provisional patent applications, the essentials about patent protection in foreign countries, tips for working with a law firm, and the tests for patent infringement.

PATENT BASICS

A patent protects an invention or discovery by giving its owner the right to exclude others from its use. In contrast, a trademark (or service mark) protects words, phrases, symbols, or designs that identify and distinguish the source of a good (or service). Copyright protects original works of authorship including literary, dramatic, musical, and artistic works, such as poetry, novels, movies, songs, computer software, and architecture.

Your invention may be marked with the notice "patent pending" once you file a patent application with the United States Patent and Trademark Office (USPTO). By comparison, any time you use a trademark or service mark, you may add the "TM" (trademark) or "SM" (service mark) designation in connection with your good or service to alert the public to your claim; you may use the federal registration symbol "®" after the USPTO actually registers the trademark or service mark. Showing a copyright notice does not require advance permission from, or registration with, the Copyright Office; the copyright notice consists of c in a circle, name of the copyright owner, and year of first publication, *e.g.,* © 2008 John Doe.

There are three types of patents. A utility patent is the most common, and it protects inventions that are functional in terms of utility, as opposed to aesthetics. A design patent protects designs that are ornamental. A plant patent protects plants that are asexually reproduced (*i.e.,* other than from seed); seeds can be protected with a certificate from the US Department of Agriculture (USDA).

Generally, the term of a new patent is 20 years from the date on which the application for the patent was filed in the United States. If the application relates to an earlier-filed application as a continuing application, the term is 20 years from the date on which the earliest such application was filed. Filing a provisional patent application before a basic, or "non-provisional," patent application effectively extends the patent term to 21 years.

The right conferred by a patent is, in the language of the statute, "the right to exclude others from making, using, offering for sale, or selling" the invention in the United States or "importing" the invention into the United States. A patent does not confer a right to make, use, or sell the invention. For example, you may need marketing approval by a regulatory authority to sell a patented drug or device. Rather, what is granted is the right to exclude; a patent is like a "no trespassing" sign. And a US patent has effect only in the US. If patent protection is required in other countries, it is necessary to file for foreign patents.

The Constitution of the United States sets forth the reasons for patenting in Article I, Section 8, by giving Congress the power "to promote the progress of science and useful arts, by securing for limited times to authors and inventors the exclusive right to their respective writings and discoveries." Under this power, Congress enacted the first patent law in 1790, with the most recent patent law being reenacted in 1952. The patent laws are now codified in Title 35 of the United States Code. The operative words from the Constitution are "limited" and "right." The Constitution authorizes these awards of a *limited right* to inventors for their discoveries in order to promote the progress of the useful arts.

What in the way of inventions and discoveries can be patented? You cannot patent a mere idea, but rather a reduction to practice of that idea. In the language of the statute, anyone who "invents or discovers" a "process, machine, manufacture, or composition of matter" or "improvement thereof" may obtain a patent. These statutory classes of subject matter taken together include, in the words of the legislative history of the 1952 Patent Act, "anything under the sun that is made by man."

The USPTO takes the position that an isolated and purified DNA molecule that has the same sequence as a naturally occurring gene is eligible for a patent because that DNA molecule does not occur in that purified or isolated form in nature. Products of nature cannot be patented because they are not "made by man." However, natural substances may constitute patentable subject matter, provided that they are "isolated and purified," because they do not occur in that "isolated" or "purified" form in nature.

The USPTO examines applications for patents to determine if the applicants are entitled to patents under the law. It grants the patents when the applicants are so entitled. The USPTO publishes patent applications 18 months from the earliest filing date, and patents are published upon issuance.

Inventorship determines ownership. The owner of the invention is the inventor; joint inventors are joint owners. Inventors usually assign their rights in the invention to the company that employs them. The entity to which the invention is assigned (*e.g.*, the company) is known as the assignee. The assignee should ensure that the assignment is recorded in the USPTO.

FORMAL REQUIREMENTS FOR GETTING A PATENT

To get a filing date, the inventors (or the assignee) must file a patent application with the USPTO that includes a specification having a description and at least one claim, drawings where necessary, an oath or declaration, and the prescribed fees. The latter two elements may be submitted late, but you will be levied a surcharge. If the inventors (or the assignee) qualify as a small entity (independent inventor, small business concern, or non-profit organization), they may claim this status and be eligible to have the Patent Office fees discounted by 50%.

The application papers must be in the English language, or an English language translation of the non-English language papers filed. The papers must be presented in a form to permit electronic reproduction, having a certain size, margins, spacing, font, font size, etc. If foreign priority (the benefit of the filing date of a prior foreign application) is claimed, you must furnish a certified copy of the priority papers before grant of the patent.

The specification must include a written description of the invention. Under contract theory, the *quid pro quo* for the patent is full disclosure. The written description requirement promotes the progress of the useful arts by ensuring that patentees adequately describe their inventions in their specifications, in exchange for the right to exclude others from copying the invention for the duration of the patent term.

The specification must enable a "hypothetical" person having ordinary skill in the art to make and use the invention. The "art" refers to the area of technology related to the invention. The invention must be enabled so that a person having ordinary skill in the art can make and use the invention without undue experimentation.

The "best mode" contemplated by the inventors of carrying out their invention must be set forth in the specification. This requirement prevents inventors from disclosing their second-best embodiment, while retaining the best for themselves. In general, to satisfy the best mode requirement, the inventors must disclose the preferred embodiments of their invention.

The specification must conclude with one or more claims. The claim or claims are required to particularly point out and distinctly claim the subject matter that the applicant regards as the invention. The claims define the scope of protection afforded by the patent, as well as the questions of patentability to be decided by the USPTO and the questions of infringement to be judged by the courts—the claims set forth the boundaries of the property being safeguarded against trespassers.

Where necessary for an understanding of the invention, drawings are required. The drawings must be presented in a form to permit electronic reproduction. The sheets of drawings must have a certain size, margins, views, etc.

Another requirement is an oath or declaration, signed by the inventors, swearing that they believe themselves to be the original and first inventors of the invention as defined by the claims. Inventorship is not the same as authorship of an academic publication. To be an inventor, the collaborator must generally contribute to the conception of the invention as claimed. Conception is "the formation in the mind of the inventor of a definite and permanent idea of the complete and operative invention as it is thereafter to be applied in practice." An inventor is not one who, although perhaps a Nobel laureate, acts solely like an encyclopedia. Neither is a laboratory technician who serves merely as a "pair of hands" an inventor. But they are inventors if they make a contribution to the conception of the invention, defined as the idea as it is to be carried out in practice and that is present in the claims.

Where the invention involves a biological material and words alone cannot sufficiently describe how to make and use the invention in a reproducible manner, access to the biological material may be necessary, in a patent depository such as at the American Type Culture Collection (ATCC).

The USPTO maintains a standardized format, called a "sequence listing," for descriptions of nucleotide and amino acid sequence data, in conjunction with the required submission of that data in computer readable form.

SUBSTANTIVE CONDITIONS FOR GETTING A PATENT

For an invention to be patentable it must be novel. Novelty means the invention must be "new" (*i.e.*, original), as well as not being precluded from patenting by what is defined in the patent law as a "statutory bar." For example, an invention cannot be patented if the invention is publicly disclosed, such as by publication of a manuscript, or commercialized, such as by offer for sale. The US provides a grace period of one year before such "statutory bars" come into play. Many countries, such as those in Europe, have no grace period. In those foreign countries, absolute novelty is required; a public disclosure before the filing date destroys patent rights.

Even if the subject matter sought to be patented is novel, and involves one or more differences from the prior art, a patent may still be refused if the differences would be obvious. In other words, to be "non-obvious" the subject matter sought to be patented must be sufficiently different from what has come before to a person having ordinary skill in the art. For example, in the original obviousness case decided by the Supreme Court of the United States in 1850, the substitution of porcelain for wood to make a doorknob was deemed to be unpatentable. The prior art was a wood doorknob. Even though the porcelain doorknob invention was novel in view of this prior art doorknob, it was nevertheless unpatentable because it would have been obvious to substitute porcelain for wood in a doorknob.

Utility, the third substantive condition, ensures that patents are granted on only those inventions that are "useful." For example, an expressed sequence tag (EST) has been held to be unpatentable for failure to be "useful" where the full length sequence of the complete gene is unknown. As another example, data from *in vitro* and animal testing are generally sufficient to support pharmacological utility in humans, if these tests would be viewed by a person having ordinary skill in the art to reasonably predict the human situation.

Under the statutory bar, patenting is precluded on an invention known or used by others in the US prior to the date of invention by the inventor; an invention patented or described in a printed publication anywhere (US or abroad) prior to the date of invention by the inventor; an invention patented or described in a printed publication anywhere (US or abroad) more than one year prior to the filing date of the patent application; an invention in public use in the US more than one year prior to the filing date of the patent application; and an invention on sale in the US more than one year prior to the filing date of the patent application.

QUIZ: WHICH OF THE FOLLOWING ARE EXAMPLES OF PUBLIC ACCESSIBILITY BY PRINTED PUBLICATION?

- The inventor presented a poster constituting 14 slides pasted on poster boards, for two and a half days, at a scientific conference.
  - Yes, the judiciary decided this is a printed publication. The moral of the story is to keep your invention secret until you file a patent application.

- The inventor presented an entirely oral presentation at a scientific conference that included neither slides nor copies of the presentation.
  - No, the judiciary decided this is not a printed

publication. Could it be a public disclosure? An oral presentation could be a public disclosure and thus be a statutory bar.

- The inventor made an oral presentation at a scientific conference that included a display of slides; a projection of the slides at the lecture was transient; and no one could be expected to remember the invention from, or take pictures of, the slides.
  - No, in 1981 the judiciary decided this is not a printed publication. How about today with cell phones? A slide show could constitute a printed publication today, due to the availability of cell phones that take pictures, and consequently be a statutory bar.

- The inventor delivered a paper orally to a scientific conference; as many as 500 attendees heard the presentation; but far less than 500 copies (approximately six copies) of the paper were distributed.
  - Yes, the judiciary decided this is a printed publication. Refer to the above moral of the story about keeping your invention secret.

- A document was posted for seven days on an Internet website and then taken down. Although the paper was accessible in a navigable directory structure, the file had a non-informative acronym name.
  - No, the judiciary decided this is not a printed publication. But the dissent argued that the paper, by being posted on the Internet on a public server for seven days, was available to anyone, and, although the file had a non-informative acronym name, was publicly accessible by virtue of a navigable directory structure. This is a close case. Refer, again, to the above moral of the story about keeping your invention secret.

SUGGESTIONS FOR PREPARING AN INVENTION DISCLOSURE

To describe a discovery sought to be patented, for technologies you develop in-house, first identify potential statutory bar dates based on past activities such as publications, abstracts, posters, talks, slide shows, manuscripts, Internet postings, grant applications, and theses and dissertations. Second, anticipate imminent statutory bar dates based on future activities. Third, describe the invention, *e.g.*, what problem(s) it solves, progressively discuss the invention in more detail, identify advantages and improvements, determine possible variations and modifications, establish competing technologies, and ascertain commercial applications. Fourth, provide data that would be required by a person having ordinary skill in the art to support the hypothesis that the invention solves the problem(s) in the prior art. Fifth, recognize who might infringe along the chain of production and among users. Sixth, determine how your competitors might design around the invention. Seventh, distinguish the relevant prior art, and discuss how it is inferior and the invention is new and improved. Eighth, indicate potential inventors. Ninth, describe the inventor's relationship with the company, *e.g.*, employee, consultant, officer. Tenth, does the government have any rights in the invention? If the invention was made with government support, (*e.g.*, a National Institutes of Health grant), the government has certain rights in the invention, including "march-in" rights. March-in rights amount to compulsory licensing, but the government has never exercised these rights.

PROVISIONAL PATENT APPLICATION FUNDAMENTALS

A provisional patent application is a "place-holder" that gives you a filing date without having to incur the cost of filing a basic or "non-provisional" patent application; by delaying the filing of a non-provisional, the inventor gets an additional year of protection and the opportunity to add data to the specification thus strengthening the patent. The provisional patent application expires 12 months after the filing date, and a non-provisional patent application claiming benefit during pendency must be filed to preserve priority. Provisional patent applications cannot themselves claim the benefit of a previously-filed application, either foreign or domestic. A provisional patent application should preferably conform to the paper size, margins, spacing, font, font size, etc. guidelines for non-provisionals; the specification must, however, comply with the written description, enablement, and best mode requirements, and refer to drawings, where necessary, for an understanding of the invention, in order to receive the benefit claimed by a later-filed non-provisional patent application. A provisional patent application can be cheaper to file than a non-provisional, because the governmental fees are considerably lower, a provisional does not need claims, and no oath or declaration is required; additionally, no costs are incurred for prosecution (getting a patent) because a provisional patent application is not examined, published, or granted.

PATENT PROTECTION IN FOREIGN COUNTRIES

Foreign patent applications should be filed within one year of the US application (whether provisional or non-provisional) so that they can claim priority from the US filing date under an international treaty called the Paris Convention (to which most industrialized nations in the world belong). There are three principal routes for foreign filing, (a) filing directly in each country, (b) filing an EPC (European Patent Convention) application, and (c) filing a PCT (Patent Cooperation Treaty) application. In the first route, national applications are filed in each country of interest. In filing an EPC application, a single EPC application is filed in the European Patent Office. Filing a PCT application consists of an international phase and a national phase. In the PCT international phase, a single international application is filed in one office (in the US), unless a foreign filing license has already been obtained, and in one language (English). In the PCT national phase, the PCT patent application is used as a vehicle to "go national," or file national applications, in each of the designated countries in which a patent is sought 30 months after the earliest filing date. About 140 countries are members of the PCT, uniting most industrialized nations in the world. Advantages of filing a PCT patent application are lower initial costs, a delay for 30 months in which to reflect on the desirability of seeking protection in foreign countries, a chance to evaluate patentability based on a "patentability report" prepared by the PCT authorities, an opportunity to amend the international application to obtain a positive patentability report, and an effective means of putting the world on notice of the application, which can assist in the watch for potential licensees. Factors to be considered in deciding the foreign countries in which to seek patent protection include the location of one's markets, competitors, and manufacturers.

TIPS FOR WORKING WITH A LAW FIRM

Registered "patent attorneys" and non-attorney "patent agents" are permitted by law to represent inventors before the USPTO. Registration means passing an examination on patent law and rules and USPTO practice and procedures and possessing a college degree in engineering or physical science or the equivalent. Both patent attorneys and agents are permitted to prepare an application for a patent and conduct the prosecution in the USPTO, but patent agents cannot conduct patent litigation in the courts or perform various services considered to be practicing law. In California, as well as other states, attorneys must have written fee agreements with their clients whenever the client's total expense, including fees, will foreseeably exceed $1,000, where the fee agreement states any basis for compensation including, but not limited to, hourly rates, flat fees, and other standard charges (*e.g.*, photocopying). For non-litigation, clients tend to pay by the hour at the firm's prevailing rates for all time spent on the client's matter by the firm's legal personnel, as opposed to litigation, where clients may negotiate payment by the hour or by a contingency fee. Many firms have moved to alternative billing for their services even for non-litigation, for example, by charging a "flat fee" that remains fixed regardless of the amount of time spent and attracts clients who wish to obtain predictability of cost and sharing of risk. The client may grant its attorney a lien for any sums owed to the attorney to attach to any patent the client may obtain, presumably as a result of the attorney's work.

THE ABCs ABOUT PATENT INFRINGEMENT

Briefly, patent infringement is defined as the unauthorized making, using, or selling, or offering to sell, the patented invention in the US, or importing of the invention into the US, during the term of the patent. You can sue for an injunction to stop the infringement or seek damages. To determine whether there is infringement, the claims will be interpreted, and the properly interpreted claims will be compared to the allegedly patented thing. Infringement requires that each and every element of the claim is found, either literally or as an equivalent, in the allegedly patented thing. Infringement may be direct, in which the actor that is sued is performing the unauthorized acts, or indirect, in which the actor that is sued is not itself performing the unauthorized acts but is contributing to it (*e.g.,* by supplying components of the allegedly patented thing) or inducing others to perform the unauthorized acts.

CONCLUSION

In conclusion, you have examined the basics about patents, formal requirements for getting a patent, substantive conditions for getting a patent, the meaning of a "statutory bar," the meaning of a "printed publication," suggestions for preparing an invention disclosure describing a discovery sought to be patented for technologies you develop in-house, the fundamentals about provisional patent applications, the essentials about patent protection in foreign countries, tips for working with a law firm, and the tests for patent infringement. Serious consideration of patent protection for your valuable inventions does not end upon the filing of a patent application. You need to reevaluate the value of your inventions during prosecution, issuance (when you pay the issue fee), and maintenance (when you pay the maintenance fees, which are due 3-½, 7-½, and 11-½ years after issue in the US). In this way, patent procurement will mediate the achievement of your quest to in-license technologies from universities and research institutes or develop technologies in-house, with the goal to out-license technologies or partner with large companies, and ultimately to commercialize new drugs and laboratory tests.

REFERENCES

1. Kenneth W. Dam, *The Economic Underpinnings of Patent Law,* 23 Journal of Legal Studies 247 (1994)

2. Joseph A. DiMasi, Ronald W. Hansen, & Henry G. Grabowski, *The Price of Innovation: New Estimates of Drug Development Costs,* 22 Journal of Health Economics 151 (2003)

3. Stuart J.H. Graham & Ted Sichelman, *Why Do Start-ups Patent?* 23 Berkeley Technology Law Journal (September 6, 2008). Available at SSRN: http://ssrn.com/abstract=1121224

CHAPTER 5

Financing Your Company

Christine Copple, PhD
CEO, Starise Ventures

Michael L. Salgaller, PhD
Biotechnology Entrepreneur, Venture Capitalist, and Medical Researcher

The latter part of the first decade of the new millennium was a very challenging time to become a biotechnology entrepreneur. It was even tough for established and serial entrepreneurs. No sector of the biotechnology value chain—from start-up to late stage—was unaffected. Whether it was an absence of money, a shortage of courage and will, or a depressed valuation environment, getting funding or securing a deal required even more skill, timing, and luck than usual. During such funding cycles—and they do run in cycles—those with money tend to become even more conservative and risk-adverse. Part of this chapter provides a snapshot of how the financing climate can be, using 2009 as the time point. The challenges and accomplishments, however, are applicable for any year. The latter part of the chapter provides some general concepts toward financing your company.

HOW CAN YOU RAISE CAPITAL AND ATTRACT PARTNERS?

Early stage investors will want to see success in securing grants to fund initial work. There are at least two reasons for this: (1) it will take less equity investment to reach a meaningful milestone, and (2) obtaining a competitive grant implies peer review and the scientific validity of the concept. Your first investors may not do the kind of in-depth due diligence later investors and partners will, so winning grant support can be a surrogate. There are multiple places to go for grants, such as the National Institutes of Health, National Science Foundation, Department of Defense, Defense Advanced Research Projects Agency (DARPA), philanthropic foundations, economic development authorities, and state venture funds. Now more than ever, the resources you secure from these efforts need to do double duty in that they must advance the technical program of the company and reduce some aspect of performance risk for the next transaction. A round of investment ought to be sufficient to carry the company to a transformative milestone that will attract either partners or investors or both. A common error is to underestimate how long that will take and hence how much it will cost. Failure to raise sufficient capital may lead to a down round that is punitive to the original investors or may drive the company to subsist on grants until the issue is resolved. This is not good management, since every month you spend waiting for the next grant is a month off the life of your patent in the marketplace, and is quietly and corrosively chewing dollars off your net present value. There are a lot of execution risks that need to be recognized and addressed before private investment has been attracted or the founder's own resources have been deployed.

Securing the firm's intellectual property in the appropriate territories and ensuring that you also have freedom to operate is key to licensing success down the road. You may be licensing the technology from an academic institution, so the terms of that license ought not to discourage subsequent partnering. If your technology is a broad platform that is not practical for a small entity to fully realize, then think about monetizing some aspect of the technology that you would otherwise be leaving on the table by licensing it to a third party.

It is never too early to consider the impact of the research and development you are undertaking on the manufacturability and regulatory path of your technology. Careful planning at this stage can avoid costly repeats later on and/or painful discounts by suitors who need to repeat work that was flawed on either front. Ideally, you want to be building a package that will be compelling and highly competitive, and not one that needs a redo.

While you are working on that package, take time to hold your own beauty contest for the partner or partners that you think will be the best fit for your drug, device or diagnostic. Get to know the kind of deals they like to do, the way they value the deals and the organizations through which they can make early bets, like a venture arm or foundation. Even before you are ready to negotiate a deal you can let them know you exist and what your time line is. If they are potentially interested, they will likely tell you at what clinical stage they would like to hear back from you, or not. Either way, it helps you create a timeline for your business development activities.

Securing a partnering or option deal with either a contract research organization or a contract manufacturing organization are options that can allow you to make technical progress, with experienced supervision, and advance your package to a more risk mitigated stage.

A partnering deal can quickly follow good clinical trial results, but usually such deals have been in the making for some time, while that trial was ongoing. Partnering deals can be structured as options pending such results, so that a serious round of funding can be teed up for when things fall into place.

The valuations of your partnerships and financing rounds will have as much to do with the state of the marketplace as they will have to do with the beauty and technical wizardry of your technology. So, opportunistic deals secured when an area is hot may be worth pursuing, even if your package is not as mature as another company in a less favored therapeutic space or technical approach.

Finally, management is a big part of the execution risk, so your team needs to be brutally frank about their strengths and weaknesses and get advisors on board who can supplement any weak spots without loading up your burn rate unnecessarily.

Let's suppose that you now have secured your IP, mapped your path to market, selected your commercialization plan and instituted studies to bring validating proof-of-principle data to the table; now what? Well you can turn all of that work into a business plan so that you will know how much money you must raise to make it happen, but you also need to go forth and pitch your opportunity to investors and partners. For that, you will need a compelling, non-confidential, one minute 'elevator pitch' and a short—around 20 slides—power point presentation and an executive one or two page 'leave behind' summary. In the event that you garner interest you will also need a longer 'use of funds' document and, ideally, an operating plan. It also helps if from the very beginning you keep all your documents that will be needed in due diligence together in organized folders which can either be posted on a secure web server or provided on a disc.

It will probably take a lot of presentations to find those first investors and partners and, given that many therapeutics take ten years to develop, you will be doing it multiple times. You should get better at it. But it is never going to be easy. It is not for the faint of heart. Nevertheless, the goal of succeeding in bringing a technology to market, and to patients in desperate need of new solutions, is an outcome that keeps many engaged.

The typical places to raise money are as follows, and are generally in the order in which a company seeks out that particular entity:

- Friends, Family, and Fools (see below, and Chapter 10)
- Angels
- Venture Capital(ists) (VCs)
- Private Placement
- Venture Philanthropy
- Venture Debt
- Hedge Funds

FRIENDS, FAMILY, AND FOOLS

Unless you are independently wealthy already you will need to turn to family, friends and fools (F3) to supplement whatever personal investment you are making in your new venture. Even F3 will expect you to put cash into the venture, as well as significant sweat equity. So, your brilliant idea alone is unlikely to swing the deal. Remember that this constituency is unlikely to be in a position to conduct significant due diligence on the technology—so they will be relying on your reading and representations. Thus, if you can, try to supplement that with third party validation and write it up as professionally as you know how. These rounds are much too small to justify the cost of legal and accounting associated with a Preferred Share deal structure. However, make sure you have corporate counsel to supervise the offering documents and write up the agreements and subscription documents. And, do not attempt to value the company at this juncture. Do the round as a Convertible Note with a coupon and warrant coverage so that it can wait out the Angel round and convert into the first round that sets a value. Alternatively, you could do it as a common share round but, if you do, realize it may be setting a low bar. Also, just because these folks like you, maybe even love you, does not mean you should not be offering them a market return. Auntie Nellie may only be looking for 20% a year but you know that the risk deserves a better return and you should build it in. Never take money from F3 if they cannot afford to lose it forever. Obviously, that is not your intent—but it is always a distinct possibility.

ANGELS

Angels are individuals or groups who invest in private, early-stage companies using their own money.[1] Often, they need to be accredited by demonstrating to an appropriate governmental oversight body that they have the financial means to make such risky investments. As a result, being an angel investor is usually limited to what are termed "high net-worth individuals." In simpler terms, it means those "rich" enough—or at least sufficiently well-off—to gamble with money they may lose completely. Accredited angel investors usually possess a net worth > $1M. From a legal standpoint, they are assumed to be sophisticated investors. Currently, there are over 200,000 angel investors in the United States across all sectors, and the billions they invest approximate the amounts put forth by venture capital firms.

Angels are often entrepreneurs themselves, who have realized a substantial return from their efforts. Biotech and biopharma angels like investing in these sectors because they feel they are doing society good—instead of just seeking a substantial return. Further, companies in these sectors are sufficiently scalable to provide a return for early-stage investors, and because many angels have accumulated their own wealth in these sectors, giving them substantive knowledge in the scientific or business aspects of these fields. This expertise distinguishes angels from regular investors and enables them to mentor, network, and actively support the businesses in which they invest.[1] Even if they are experienced in business and technology, they are not typically experts of the financial instruments and legal contracts necessary to do the deal—so always have a financial professional and attorney involved.

Angel groups have become more common, replacing individuals to some extent. Angel groups provide the social interaction and teamwork not present when working alone. It is also easier to have greater deal flow via a social network. From a business standpoint, there is shared risk and smarter investing, as angels can work together on "due diligence." (The background check on a potential investment is commonly known by this term.) Pooled funds also allow investors to have greater and longer impact in the development of technologies. It puts them in a stronger bargaining position when subsequent, larger investors—primarily VCs—enter the picture.

Angel groups and networks are most often found within 150-mile radius of major metropolitan areas.[2] The range of funds typically available varies widely, from as little as $10K to many millions. However, it is unusual for an angel group to collectively invest less than $100K. In general, angels seek a 40-50% internal rate of return (IRR)—which translates to 3-5X their investment over 3 years. Angels and angel groups thus fill a critical gap in equity financing for early-stage businesses between raising money from friends and family and venture capital. They are often not as rigorous as VCs when performing due diligence on the potential investment. They tend not to be as rigorous on valuation and other deal terms. Also simplifying matters for the early-stage company, the deal documents are more limited in scope, and angels typically assume no board role or hands-on, active involvement.

Angel rounds are often done as convertible debt wherein money goes in accumulating a fixed interest rate and, at a time in the future, can be converted into equity in whole or in part. The first advantage to the angel is that debt is senior to equity in the event of a wind-down (i.e., ceasing operations) so that the holders of debt are paid out of any liquidation resources first. The second advantage is that the angel does not need to set a firm valuation on the company at the time of the investment. Instead, the deal usually provides a discounted conversion to the valuation set at the next round of financing when a VC will likely do a professional valuation. The angel gets the discount in recognition of the fact that he took the risk at an earlier stage and helped to reduce the execution risk for the incoming investment through that commitment. Both the angel and the company benefit for the inclusion of warrants in the deal, since this produces an additional influx of capital for the company at a later date and the angel gets an additional 'sweetened' opportunity to up their investment if things are going well. (Warrants allow an investor to buy an additional, proportionate amount of common or preferred stock at a fixed price sometime in the future. This fixed price remains constant even as the value of the company and its stock options increases.)

Angels usually will not seek as high a percentage of company ownership/equity for their investment as venture capital firms. Though less equity for the money is good for the entrepreneur and the early-stage company, the amount of capital able to be raised from angels is usually insufficient to get to a liquidity event (i.e., merger, acquisition, or initial public offering) or the marketplace. Further, most angels may not have the biotech business, financial, technical, or commercialization expertise to bring substantial "value-add" besides the cash itself.

So, where do you find angels? Ah, not an easy answer, for they are everywhere and nowhere. Although numerous, they are often hard to find. They do not advertise, have websites, or seek attention that would make entrepreneurs bother them. If you are still on the faculty of a medical research or university—or maintain affiliations or networks—the technology transfer office (or licensing office) is a good place to start. Depending upon its sophistication and resources, such offices may be able to directly channel an executive or technology summary to an angel or angel network. They will submit it to those with whom they have a good, professional relationship—whether in your geographic area or not. It is a actually a good thing if the university staffer making the connection is hesitant to reveal information about the investor; again, anonymity puts the angel in a more positive frame of mine since they prefer dealing with more sophisticated tech transfer offices … it lends an air of confidence and comfort before they even receive your materials. If the university has a business school, they may be connected as well. Though the business school likely has more connections outside of the life sciences sector—simply because a higher percentage of investors do not get involved with it—it is still worth trying. There may be school alumni that, having done well in their chosen profession, are giving back to their alma mater. Some give back via endowing chairs or putting up buildings, while others put their money into ideas and dreams.

There are also organizations that specialize in best practices for angels such as the Angel Capital Association, which represents over sixty angel groups, and the Capital Formation Institute, which promotes networking and deal flow through its website at http://www. cfi-institute.org. There are also regional meetings, such as World's Best Technology held each year in Texas. There is even a foundation dedicated to promoting entrepreneurship—the Ewing Marion Kauffman Foundation—and much can be learned from their website, http://www.Kauffman.org, and their many publications.

Service providers (*e.g.*, law firms, accounting firms, and consultants) can be a good source of contacts. In fact, whether a service provider has—and, importantly, is willing to make—connections, should be part of your due diligence when looking for help in matters involving the law, accounting, insurance, etc. Trust their judgment as far as the proper time to make an introduction—if they present you before you're ready, you and the provider look foolish, and the investor gets annoyed and less amenable to similar gestures in the future. Your affiliated technology transfer office or economic development agency should be able to supply potential service providers: it is certainly understandable that the newly-minted (or newly-contemplating) entrepreneur needs help finding service providers as an initial step before seeking investor contacts. And speaking of economic development agencies, such entities are additional sources for angel information. All states have economic/business development agencies; many have divisions or departments specifically focused on life sciences or biotechnology. If you live in an area with a strong, vibrant life sciences community, your region, county, or city may also have its own economic development entities. If you are unsure, then begin at the state level.

A recurring theme of this book—as well as a separate chapter—is the importance of networking. Not surprisingly, this is true as well when looking for funding. Attend whatever investment fairs and forums, pitch sessions, boot camps, coaching sessions, etc., your area offers. At such educational and networking events, seek out referrals from other entrepreneurs. See who is speaking, on the panels, and in attendance. Seek them out and gently approach them for information.

Finally, you can look for information and contacts via the web. As previously indicated, almost all individual angels, and many angel groups/networks, aren't accessible this way. If they have a website, there is usually minimal information provided. If they have a website that allows submissions by entrepreneurs, it is usually via an "info@" kind of web portal. Going through an anonymous web portal is the computer version of cold-calling. Consequently, it is also the least effect. Doing so is unlikely to be successful, so if you decide to submit your company documents/information this way, be sure to make it one part of a more comprehensive and direct strategy.

You should approach angels largely the same way as venture capitalists or other more professional investors (as compared with friends and family). Briefly, do your homework beforehand: be ready to explain how your deal fits into the angels' investment focus. Have an executive summary that includes the value proposition, plus all key elements (target market, products, IP, competition, team, etc.). It is likely that the process towards a go/go-no decision whether they invest is also similar (if somewhat less formal) to VCs: pitch meeting, due diligence, deal term negotiations, deal documents. Facilitate due diligence for angels to reach the decision point sooner, as angels will not spend as much time and resources as VCs. Although deal negotiations and documents may not be as standardized as with VCs, expect such steps and time requirements when planning your schedule to raise capital.

VENTURE CAPITAL

Venture capital firms are companies that primarily make investments on behalf of others—rather than themselves; hence, one key distinction from angel groups. It is not unusual for those running the firm to use some of their own money—but most usually comes from elsewhere. Money is typically collected ("raised") from wealthy people (also known as "high net-worth individuals) and institutions such as state retirement systems, insurance companies, and mutual funds. Large amounts of money (from tens to hundreds of millions) are pooled in what are referred to as "funds." Investments are made out of such funds. A management fee (typically 2-3% annually) is charged to manage the funds. This is a similar arrangement to that of a financial planner or similar professional putting your money in various investment vehicles and products. In this instance, the VC is facilitated and directing investment, and the investment is in individual biotechnology companies instead of stocks and bonds. Your technology and management team are the commodity being invested into, rather than oil, gold, or corn.

In exchange for their money, VCs want two things: (1) a piece of your company ("equity"), and (2) involvement. In some cases, they will want big enough piece of your company (>50%) to take majority control. In some cases, their involvement—the degree of which depends upon how their firm operates—will seem like an additional, more hands-on way of taking control. Often, they will want at least one seat on your board of directors. Sometimes, they will want a majority of seats. VCs may only be in contact during semi-annual or quarterly board meetings. Or, they may call and email you constantly. It depends on the firm and the individual in the firm overseeing the investment.

Many entrepreneurs fear and resist VCs and their money. Either they've experienced a negative situation themselves, or heard horror stories second-hand. They don't want to give up any significant piece of what they've founded—let alone a majority interest. They fear being manipulated, taken advantage of, abused, and bossed around. They will tell you what experiments to run and which markets to exploit—both of which differ from your original ideas. (And, of course, you know more than they do.) They will take over the daily operations and decision-making process. They will even kick you out of your firm on a whim, replacing you with someone they like better. And, as a final indignity, when the times comes for everyone to get rich (i.e., company is sold or goes public [usually via an initial public offering of stock]), you'll be forced to watch helplessly as most of the cash goes to the VCs and their minions. This is a limited and limiting viewpoint—although it can be accurate as well! Nonetheless, as a result, you may have already resolved to do everything you can to avoid taking VC money. I would strongly advise you not to close this door before even exploring what it may lead to. Looking into a VC investment should be part of your overall corporate and funding strategy. The ultimate decision whether to take VC money is yours. The factors influencing the decision are many, and may make you feel as though you're being forced into a decision you don't want. As they sometimes say in the business about taking VC investment: it depends how bad you need the money. Still, the ultimate decision is yours, and you need to take ownership of this responsibility by doing your homework ("due diligence") about VCs in general and each firm in particular.

You just may find that VCs can provide cash at a fair exchange value, guide rather than control, nurture rather than take over, and include you to a significant degree when it's time for everyone to get rich. Any good investment partner will bring substantial "value-add" in addition to the money itself. The value-add could be on the business side. You could tap into their network of proven service providers, experts, and advisors. The value-add could be on the technical side. You could tap into their network of industry professionals who've successful gotten products in your sector to the marketplace. (Most entrepreneurs know academic thought-leaders, rather than those who have actually taken a product through the regulatory process and onto the customer. This is a key distinction.) Chances are you'll need more money at some point. A good VC firm will introduce you to follow-on investors, and may even participate in additional financing rounds. Remember that they, like you, are in this to make money. Sure, they probably like and respect you. But, more importantly, they have a financial obligation to their investors to maximize financial returns. If you are smart and careful, you will align your interests with theirs in order to maximize your financial return. Here's a very important concept many entrepreneurs fail to realize when it comes to the matter of control: it's better to own a small percentage of a success than a large percentage of a failure.

To some degree, whether you end up with a success or horror story largely depends upon how well you know with whom you're dealing. Speak with principals at existing "portfolio companies" (i.e., other investments they've made). Speak with business professionals in your region, including other investors. Speak with anyone who may know anything. Keep in mind that you would be entering a business relationship that, due to the lengthy time-lines inherent with most biotechnology products, will last many years. Why would you enter into a binding relationship—legally, finally, and personally—without really knowing the other party? And isn't is highly preferable to do so with someone you like, believe in, and trust? Thus, you need to do similarly extensive due diligence about each VC firm you may deal with as they are doing on their end.

Here's a brief aside as to why VCs need to take some degree of equity and control. The following is meant as an explanation, not a justification. A VC investment is the worst of all worlds when it comes to an investment: (1) high-risk, (2) long-term, and (3) illiquid. It is an incredible risk, as the percentage of biotechnology companies that fail to make any money at anytime during their existence is huge. Many other types of investments (e.g., real estate or restaurants) may at least make some money before going under. Not so with biotechnology firms, most of which never have revenue—let alone profit. Second, it is a long-term process. Most therapeutics require >5 years to get to the market or reach some other way to get a return on investment. It still takes >3 years for most devices, diagnostics, or tools. Finally, other, more traditional types of investments provide a greater return the longer it is left alone, as well as the less you have access to it ("liquidity"). Not so with a VC investment. They can't get their money for a long time, and can't get it out if they change their mind ("illiquid"). Given such conditions, it is sometimes a wonder that anyone does biotech investment in the first place. Perhaps—if you look at the situation through their eyes (and wallets)—you may begin to understand the lengths they sometimes need to go to protect their investment and, in their eyes, tip the balance towards a favorable outcome.

So, if you decide to consider taking their money, you'll need to find them. The places and methods to find VCs are similar to those for angels and other investors. Try to secure a personal introduction. Here are 10 to get you started:

1. Call your chamber of commerce and ask if it hosts a venture capital group. Many such groups have a chamber affiliation.
2. Call a regional or state Economic Development Department or Small Business Development Center near you and ask the executive director if they know of any investor groups. Ask the U.S. Small Business Administration if you need to locate such entities.
3. Ask your accountant. If your accountant does not know, call a one of the "Big Five: accounting firms. Ask for the partner handling entrepreneurial services to point you in the right direction.
4. Ask your attorney. They should know who has money.
5. Call a professional angel investor (or group) and ask if he or she is aware of a venture capitalist group.
6. Websites, such as the National Venture Capital Association (www. nvca.org)
7. Call the editor of a local business publication; these professionals often write about such activity.
8. Look at the "Principal Shareholders" section of initial public offering (IPO) prospectuses for companies in your area. This will tell you who has had successful exits from previous investments, and thus possess the cash you can tap into.
9. Call the executive director of a trade association; preferably, one you belong to. Ask if there are any investors who specialize in your industry.
10. Ask your banker. If a small bank, ask the president of the institution. If a larger commercial bank, ask your lender. If you do not have a lender, ask for a lender who works with loans of $1 million or less. A good small-business banker knows of such groups because companies that have received an equity investment are good candidates for a loan.

You want to target firms that are a strategic fit. You'll need a firm that truly does seed- and early-stage investment. Many claim they do, but "early" to them means early in the clinical trial process. Be sure they invest in your sector, be it drugs, devices, services, diagnostics, or tools. Be sure they invest in your geography. The stereotype of the VC who doesn't like to get on a plane (for board meetings or face-to-face meetings with portfolio companies) has more than a grain of truth. Again, you can figure out what each firm's strategy via their website, current portfolio companies, and asking those in the know. If possible, start before you need to raise money (*e.g.*, "I don't need your money now, but thought you'd be interested to learn more"). Such an approach permits developing relationships and trust prior to asking for money.

PRIVATE PLACEMENT

At some point in the process of fund raising it may be suggested that you consider hiring a private placement firm to secure the next round. Typically, these firms will charge an engagement fee or retainer deposit plus monthly fees and expenses and then will garner a percentage of the round of financing upon completion. That percentage tends to follow how challenging the environment is and can range from 3% to 10%. In addition, this fee is usually supplemented with a similar percentage of warrant coverage with discounted face value and five or more years to exercise. This can be a very effective way to raise money in 6 to 12 months but it can also be a very effective way to use up what little money you have to no avail. Private placement firms can help you write a compelling private offering memorandum (PPM) and groom you and your presentation for the best impact. Nevertheless, that PPM should be partially drafted and certainly vetted by corporate counsel and your accounting firm. The placement firm should also be getting you in front of a constant stream of prospective investors who would have a genuine interest in your particular opportunity. If you choose to try this route, it is critically important to research the firms you consider and talk with previous clients. Firms will give you contacts for reference due diligence, but most will only provide ones for firms where they succeeded in securing funding. This exercise may seem like an expensive way to raise money. However, if you have a potential $400 MM per year asset which will lose an extra six months of useful patent life without the help, then, over the long haul, it can be a good investment.

Along the way of funding your operations you are likely to detect that you might miss a key milestone deadline which would put you at risk of a down round. Before that happens, it might be prudent to look for a bridge from where you are to where you will need to be to actually reach that transformative milestone. Bridge funding is typically done as convertible debt with a fixed coupon and a fairly short lifespan of a year or so. To compensate for the high risk of such a vehicle, there is generous warrant coverage, plus a discount on the conversion of the debt into the next round. That conversion might also include a sliding component, in that the longer it takes you to complete the milestone and secure the next round, the higher the discount to match the risk with the return. Existing investors are a good source of such bridging—but so are VCs who might be looking to go in on the next round, or even lead it, when you hit your milestone. While this, too, may seem like expensive money, it is much cheaper than the alternative.

VENTURE PHILANTHROPY

Perhaps the newest source of funding is venture philanthropy—also called "social entrepreneurism." It is an approach to accelerate the pace of product development from bench to bedside to marketplace. It applies principals traditionally practiced by the enthusiastic forces of capitalism, venture capitalists, to those involved with charitable giving. It puts formally disparate aims in alignment. For the foundation, the aim is getting medical products to their patient community. For the entrepreneur, the aim is getting medical products to the marketplace. In reality, these are one and the same. Venture philanthropy is a recent concept and, as with the earliest years of any new funding program, competition for such monies is lower than it will be as the decade progresses. Most entrepreneurs do not seek foundation dollars once they have started their companies—even if the academic group they came from receives grants from those entities—mistakenly believing that the flow of support stops once commercialization enters the picture. This notion was accurate, up until the last decade of the 20th century. Today, the choices for funding have expanded, and early-stage companies should add foundations to their funding strategy.

At its most basic, venture philanthropy is the funding of for-profits by not-for-profits. Venture philanthropy brings charitable giving under the same guidelines as more traditional sources of early capital, such as angel investment and venture capital. Those guidelines involve strategies, skills, and resources not previous applied to medical research. Sure, a typical academically-oriented research grant has a schedule, as well as goals/aims to be accomplished during certain periods of time. However, what are the consequences of not adequately addressing or accomplishing all the goals of an academic grant? Usually, the answer is either: (a) none, (b) write another grant, or (c) both! Ask most academic researchers for a list of short- (*e.g.*, weekly) and long-term (*e.g.*, quarterly) deadlines and associated milestones, and they will look at you like you forgot to take your medication. In stark contrast, what are the consequences of not adequately addressing or accomplishing all the goals of a venture philanthropy grant? Often, the response is a cessation in cash flow, irreversible damaging of the relationship, and the distinct likelihood of never receiving support again.

Okay; unlike some angel or venture investors, foundations will not shut down your company as the price of not doing what you said you would do within the time you promised to do it. However, just because they are not looking for a 5-10-fold internal rate of return does not mean their money is not as precious to them as any full-blooded capitalist. Thus, venture philanthropy is centered on principals that will ring familiar to entrepreneurs: importance of a driven and focused leadership, game-changing ideas, strong internal and out-sourced support, and dynamic board involvement. Although most foundations rarely take voting board seats due to the fiduciary and potential conflict-of-interest implications, they will still conduct due diligence on who serves.

Though how venture philanthropy is conducted varies by organization, some common threads exist. It is a relatively recent concept in that, traditionally, foundations and similar not-for-profits funded academic medical research. Patient communities, advocacy groups, and their 'trade associations' (foundations) are increasingly dissatisfied with the "bang for the buck" they have been getting from traditional academic grant support. Increasingly, foundations grew increasing aware of a basic problem with the traditional way of doing business: too few of their precious dollars was translating to treatments for the patients they supported, advocated for, lobbied for, and sometimes saw in their own families. Sure, it was significant to fund basic research and career-development awards at universities and medical centers. However, by focusing entirely and predominantly on the basic research into a disease, foundations all but guaranteed it would be at least a decade before any of such work progressed to patients. They look to venture philanthropy to get treatments, diagnostics, etc., to those they represent, with the same urgency they feel on a daily basis.

Herceptin®, the FDA-approved treatment for HER-2+ breast cancer, represents a good illustrative example. It was almost 15 years from the time that the genetic cause of this breast cancer subset was discovered until Herceptin®—an antibody specifically targeting the abnormality—was approved by the FDA. So, while it is genuinely a proud breakthrough for a foundation to announce that they supported the research that discovered the gene causing a disease, that pride now comes with the daunting knowledge of the incredible length of time until any patient directly benefits. To those dealing with any quality- or quantity-of-life illness, 15 years from discovery to application is unacceptable. Consider a highly progressive childhood disease, with terrible morbidity and mortality. What good is a treatment in 10 or 15 years when most current patients will be untreatable or dead before they get out of their teens? Faced with such difficult questions, foundations decided something different had to be done. And what many foundations decided that "something different" meant moving later (i.e., downstream) in the product development process in considering what entities to support. It also meant aligning their interests with those motivated to go in a straight line from answer to answer—not off in tangents from question to question. That meant aligning their interests with the for-profit world, and ending the complete dismissal of those pursuing the greater good just because it was connected with making money.

Entrepreneurs, as well as those involved in start-up biotechs should always keep in mind what "value-add" an investor may or may not bring. That is, how can they help your company grow and succeed, in addition to their money? The same perspective is used when looking toward a foundation for funding. Although different from traditional investors, they bring the potential of unique benefits. Those foundations large enough to be involved in venture philanthropy likely have expanded beyond the patient community origins to include in-house scientific and/or medical expertise. Consequently, companies awarded funding can justifiably claim at least a threshold level of technical validation by an objective, outside party. The larger the foundation, the more significant and substantial their scientific/medical/clinical advisory boards. It is not uncommon for several key thought-leaders on a particular disease or condition to be formally affiliated with one or more foundations addressing that particular disease or condition. The input they provide is at least as useful—often more so due to greater transparency—than reviewers' comments on a typical grant from federal or state agencies.

One advantage of foundation support can be the access they can provide to clinical trials networks and the patient recruitment associated with them. For example, the Cystic Fibrosis Foundation (CFF) has a wholly-owned subsidiary called Cystic Fibrosis Foundation Therapeutics (CFFT), which supports drug discovery and development. This arm of the foundation spends tens of millions a year on supporting early stage pre-clinical and clinical development. Their virtual pipeline of drugs get valuable financing at that most challenging of stages in discovery and development. CFF has been among the trailblazers of this approach and are now highly sophisticated of venture philanthropy bringing money, know-how and patients to the table. Along the way, organizations like this have learned to participate in equity and obtain reach in rights. The success of the company can realize equity gains for the foundation which can be ploughed back into programs advancing other solutions. The ability of the foundation/inventor/licensor to regain access to the technology ("reach-in rights") can protect patients' access to technology if the company fails to advance the program either through lack of execution or through business or financing failure.

Not all foundations are interested in venture philanthropy. Many remain committed to supporting the more traditional academic setting. How do you know whether they support for-profit entrepreneurship? Not surprisingly, websites are a good place to start. Take a look at the types of research for which funding is provided. The Health Research Alliance (www.healthra.org), a consortium of non-governmental funders of medical research, has a venture philanthropy initiative and can supply helpful input. Size is not the complete story. Many large charities (*e.g.*, Avon Foundation, Multiple Myeloma Research Foundation, Michael J. Fox Foundation, and Juvenile Diabetes Research Foundation) offer millions or tens of millions per year. However, smaller charities for rare diseases may only provide a few grants each funding cycle—yet still include for-profits as valid candidates. The grant amounts vary widely from a few thousand dollars—enough to defray part of the expense of a proof-of-concept lab experiment—to many millions—enough to cover all costs of a Phase I (i.e., 'first-in-human') clinical trial. A great resource for learning about foundations in your space is the website GuideStar.org, which is a searchable database of almost all philanthropic organizations in the country. With a premium registration you can get exquisite details of the amounts raised, or endowments owned, how the money is spent, and on what, as well as the names and contact information for officers. Such registration can be purchased by the month or year, and is an excellent place to start your search. When you travel to professional conferences, seek out the foundations and patient advocacy groups. At larger meetings, they will be placed in their own section of the exhibit hall. At smaller, more defined meetings, they may be major sponsors—in which case they will be well-represented. Travel outside the usual academically-oriented talks and posters; get out there and meet those outside your comfort and familiarity zone. The benefits can be substantial.

As with any potential funding source, you need to do your homework. The specific aims of your research must be in alignment with the goals of the foundation of interest. It is not a deal-breaker if your company's lead indication is different from their patient focus. In fact, it could be used to expand your pipeline without much additional outlay of precious resources. You could explore the potential benefit of a secondary indication for a lead product, or a primary indication of a follow-on product. For example, if your product addressed a gastrointestinal-based autoimmune condition—such as irritable bowel syndrome—it might also be used to address a musculoskeletal-based autoimmune condition—such as multiple sclerosis. Once you have identified some target foundations, an in-person visit can be quite helpful. Most foundations have MDs and PhDs either on staff or as affiliates. Sitting across the table at their headquarters provides the chance to discuss areas of mutual interest. Have several potential projects as discussion points. Foundation representatives will indicate which ideas are of greatest interest—*those* projects should be the focus of your grant submission. Receiving input from the foundation as to what and where *their* interests lie is like getting clues to a mystery—the mystery being what types of research/technology are being funded. Let them know you will be submitting a grant and that they should keep an eye out for it. Mention your face-to-face meeting in your grant cover letter. You have already established the seeds of a relationship—continue to nurture and tend to it.

Thus, seeking venture philanthropy money should be a fundamental part of most biotech start-ups' financing strategy. And, if fortunate enough to get a foundation grant, make it a prominent part of your introductory presentations/conversations with investors. Such funding is usually non-dilutive capital, and represents further validation of your ideas. Thus, such an accomplishment should be front and center.

VENTURE DEBT AND HEDGE FUNDS

These two sources of capital are rarely available to start-up and early-stage biotechnology firms—especially those in the therapeutic, device, or diagnostic space. Therefore, more than an introduction is not germane to the intended audience of this book. (The situation is a bit less cut-and-dry for companies in the tools or research reagents/supplies sectors. These markets do not require much, if any, regulatory input. Consequently, their [significantly shorter] time-lines and [greatly lower] cost to reach the marketplace is not problematic to venture debt firms and hedge funds.)

Venture debt is the general term for any type of loan provided to a firm that still requires venture capital to keep moving forward and the doors open. Typical uses of funds include: major equipment, bridge financing, and general (albeit major) corporate activities. A certain amount of money is made available for a finite period of time, and the company can access any or all such funds during this "draw period." The repayment period is relatively quick: often 12 to 36 months. The financial terms can be steep—but in a different fashion than with VCs. Unlike VCs, venture debt firms get their return on investment from interest rates charged on the borrowed money—much like a loan your bank might provide to buy a car or add an addition to your home. They will rarely take equity, especially in lieu of a percentage return within a defined time period. A lien against assets—often IP—is usually required. Given that IP is the major asset of early-stage biotech, this is a risky source of capital. Venture debt is most often available for companies with revenue, or pre-revenue firms that have received at least an initial (i.e., Series A) round of VC financing.

Hedge funds are very large investment firms that typically hold on to investments for days or weeks rather than years. They are most often involved with public firms, as the amount of minimum capital they invest (usually tens of millions) puts them way out of the smaller amounts needed by start-up biotechs.

SNAPSHOT: THE VENTURE FUNDING ENVIRONMENT IN 2009

The flow of venture funding every year has been tracked since 1995 by the MoneyTree Report, compiled by the National Venture Capital Association and the accounting firm PricewaterhouseCoopers. If you want access to all the data, it is available[3]. For a snapshot of the financial environment in which entrepreneurs were recently operating, all you need are some highlights.

The MoneyTree Report year-end assessment for 2009 was that venture investment as a whole hit the lowest levels in more than a decade with dollars placed reaching only $17.7 billion across all sectors. One would have to go back to 1997 to find a similar total. This was a substantial 37% drop in dollars invested and a 30% reduction in deals over 2008—which was itself a down year.

Early in 2009, the money that was flowing was going into expansion and later-stage operations that might be anticipated to land a business development deal at their next inflection point or as a result of an option deal consummation. And, first time financings hit their lowest level since 1995. By the end of the fourth quarter, as activity ticked up slightly, seed and early-stage companies were again getting attention and none too soon either. But, this increase in enthusiasm for new and/or early bets was offset by a decline in commitments to expansion and later stage deals. By year-end biotechnology had suffered a 19% decline in dollars invested, although the $3.5 billion invested in 406 deals made it the largest sector. Biotechnology, combined with medical devices, garnered 34% of all venture investment dollars versus a 28% share in 2008. So, investment in life sciences fell, but not as so much as in cleantech and software!

WHAT WERE THE REASONS FOR THESE SLOWDOWNS?

Clearly, a good deal of caution was fuelled by concerns generated by the overall economy. The weak and uncertain economic outlook, on an international scale, made the prospects for venture funds raising new capital mixed at best. Those that did so may have given their limited partners better terms than in the past, in order to close the new funds. For example, for their new sixth fund Polaris Ventures lowered its carried interest from 30% to 20% and added a return hurdle to recapture higher carry if earned. Meanwhile, the weak exit environment, with the public offering market unstable or closed, generated demand on existing funds by top portfolio companies for ongoing operations. Funds had to pick and choose who to support and who not to support.

WHY IS THIS IMPORTANT TO ENTREPRENEURS?

Don't entrepreneurs usually start their businesses with personal stakes, along with friends, family and fools capital? Well, yes they do; however, if you want to be able to go to family Thanksgiving dinner five years from now you might want to give these early adopters a good return rather than a good drubbing. Hence, right from the very start of your new endeavor you need to consider what you will need to look like to attract capital, of ever increasing sophistication, as you build your company. What inflection point might need to be achieved to encourage angels to invest? How long will it take to get to that point and can you secure enough seed capital to get there? What will the next inflection point be? How long and how much will it take to get there? And, then what will the capital markets look like when you are ready and what might that mean for your valuation and trajectory? This does not mean that you will be in control, but it will give you a game plan to adjust as better data comes in and feedback is secured. It will also help protect you from over optimism and the resulting under capitalization.

A LOOK BACK AT THE PRIVATE DEALS & IPOS OF 2009

In trying to answer these questions it can be instructive to look at the deals completed in this most challenging of years. So, we took a look at 70 private deals to try to garner some insights. Below we discuss some selected examples that illustrate key characteristics found in many of these deals.

January saw the $50 million preferred stock financing for Anacor Pharmaceuticals, which included not only venture capital investors, but also two pharmaceutical companies GlaxoSmithKline (GSK) and Schering Corporation. This coming together of interests no doubt helped to secure the round for Anacor which is developing a boron chemistry platform for topical anti-fungals and anti-inflammatories as well as systemic anti-infectives. Their pipeline of products ranges from pre-clinical through Phase II clinical trials.

Also in January, Intradigm secured the final tranche of its $21.4 million Series B round for their targeted, systemic RNAi therapeutics platform and delivery technology aimed at oncology. Participating in the round with current investors was Lilly Ventures. That same month Hydra Biosciences secured a $22 million Series D round of financing from venture sources. Hydra is developing ion-channel drugs for pain, inflammation and pulmonary applications that avoid narcotic side effects. Their platform leverages discoveries in the Transient Receptor Potential family channels which present 'first in class' drug opportunities in major unmet therapeutic markets. They have four compounds in pre-clinical development. Among their venture investors are MedImmune Ventures, Biogen Idec New Ventures and

Lilly Ventures.

In February Kythera Biopharmaceuticals secured an additional $10 million when their investors triggered an early exercise of their Series C secured investment rights in which all their current investors participated. Kythera is developing novel products for aesthetic dermatology and has completed one Phase II trial and two Phase I trials. Their management team is heavily weighted with Amgen alumni. Mpex Pharmaceuticals closed $27.5 million of a projected $40 million Series D financing to move their antibiotic Aeroquin® through Phase 2b trials and into Phase III trials for cystic fibrosis. The company is developing a pipeline of inhibitors of multi-drug resistant efflux pumps in a world wide alliance with GSK. Also in February, Sopherion Therapeutics closed a $55 million Series C round for their anti-cancer non-pegylated liposomal doxorubicin (Myocet™M) which is going into global Phase III trials for first line therapy in HER-2 over-expressing metastatic breast cancer patients. The lead investor was Zoticon BioVentures which is a global drug development and healthcare investment entity. Zoticon had previously in-licensed Myocet™ in 2008 and was joined in this round by half a dozen venture capital firms. February also saw the regenerative medicine company Garnet Biotherapeutics raise $10.4 million for their programs to speed healing and reduce scarring after surgery in dermatological procedures. The company plans to use the resources to advance their Phase II clinical trials of proprietary human adult bone marrow-derived cells and to develop manufacturing capacity.

In March, Proteon Therapeutics closed the first $38 million of a Series B round of financing for their end stage renal disease surgical arteriovenous fistula (AVF) patient indication. In addition, the firm closed an exclusive option with Novartis whereby Novartis can acquire Proteon after a successful completion of Phase II clinical trials. The total deal has a projected potential value of $550 million. When the indication garnered orphan drug designation in May a further $12 million was invested by existing and new venture investors. Another March deal was the $20 million Series A Preferred round of Regulus Therapeutics by its founding investors Alnylam Pharmaceuticals and Isis Pharmaceuticals, which had previously set up Regulus as a joint venture. Regulus focuses on microRNAs, which are the master regulators of the genome, and has over 600 issued and 300 pending patents around this space. A month after the financing closed the company announced an alliance with GSK to study microRNAs in immuno-inflammatory diseases and, in February, 2010, they announced a Hepatitis C deal with GSK worth $150 million plus royalties. Another March deal was Reata Pharmaceuticals which brought in a $32 million round to fund a Phase 2b trial of bardoxolone methyl, a member of the anti-oxidant inflammation modulators (AIMs) family, for chronic kidney disease and Type 2 Diabetes. This is a small orally available molecule administered once a day. Reata has a pipeline of compounds capable of addressing a very broad range of indications from renal to cardiovascular, auto-immune, CNS, pulmonary and cancer. This same month, Sangart completed their Series F funding round for a total of $50 million raised from existing investors. The raise resulted from the exercise of warrants issued during their 2007 Series F round of financing. As a result their F round generated a total of $100 million. The company is using the capital to fund further clinical development of their MP4 oxygen transport therapeutic products. The warrant exercise followed positive results in a Phase III trial of Hemospan for hypotension in hip replacement procedures but was also preceded by a reduction in force and management reorganization as well. By year-end the company had secured E.U. orphan medicinal product designation for MP4CO for sickle cell disease. Another early, large, deal was Victory Pharma's $45 million raise for their pipeline in pain management which contains two Phase III drugs and three Phase II drugs. The company already has four approved drugs in the market and also plans to expand through product acquisitions.

April saw Synageva Biopharma Corp. raise $30 million for further development of their therapies for rare diseases and unmet medical needs as well as their proprietary Synageva Expression Platform (SEP™) for monoclonal antibody development and production. In July, they announced a collaboration with Morphotek Inc. (a subsidiary of Eisai Corporation of North America) to develop potential treatments for cancer and infectious disease including enhanced manufacturing for antibodies currently in Phase II and Phase III clinical trials at Morphotek for cancer. By the fourth quarter they had raised an additional $15 million to make their 2009 round a total of $45 million. Another early second quarter deal was Applied Genetic Technologies which raised $11.8 million. The firm is focused on genetic therapies and has two Phase I trials ongoing for genetic therapy in orphan diseases. They also have a collaboration with Genzyme for wet age-related macular degeneration.

May saw Avid Radiopharmaceuticals raise $34.5 million in a Series D round that included Pfizer Venture Investments and Lilly Ventures. The company aims to change the medical management of significant chronic human diseases by detecting disease at its earliest stages before serious symptoms emerge using their new molecular imaging agents. Their pipeline includes a Phase III for Alzheimers disease, a Phase II for Parkinson's disease and a Phase I program in diabetes. Calistoga Pharmaceuticals raised a $30 million B round in May for the development of their isoform-selective phosphoinositide 3-kinase (PI3K) inhibitors for the treatment of cancer and inflammatory diseases. And, Vaxinnate closed their Series D round of $30 million with investors that included MedImmune Ventures, Oxford Bioscience Partners and The Wellcome Trust. Vaxinnate's technology aims to dramatically improve the potency, manufacturing capacity and cost effectiveness of vaccines; an agenda well in sync with the investors' agendas. Cempra Pharmaceuticals closed a $46 million Series C financing to further fund their clinical and pre-clinical programs in oral antibiotics. And, Elixir Pharmaceuticals raised $12 million on the heels of their Option Agreement for their pre-clinical oral ghrelin antagonist with Novartis that could eventually be worth $500 million.

In July Presidio Pharmaceuticals announced a further $27 million into their $54.5 million round to further the development of their novel, validated small molecule anti-viral therapeutics for Hepatitis C and HIV. This same month the transdermal delivery company Zosano Pharma succeeded in raising $30 million on the heels of positive Phase II results for their needle free, transdermal patch delivery system for osteoporosis. And, NanoBio Corporation increased its Series B raise from $12 million to $22 million with an additional investment by Perseus LLC. The company is developing a nanoemulsion-based intranasal vaccine technology as well as dermatological and anti-infective products.

Chimerix closed their $16.1 million Series E round of financing in August with a group of leading life science venture capital investors. The company is developing orally available anti-viral therapeutics by leveraging their proprietary phospholipid intramembrane microfluidization conjugate technology with existing anti-viral compounds. They are currently in Phase II trials. August was a very exciting month as it also saw the IPO of Cumberland Pharmaceuticals on the NASDAQ exchange which went out at $17 per share to raise $85 million. The company has several products already in the marketplace including Caldolor which is an intravenous ibuprofen formulation for pain and fever that gained FDA approval in June of 2009. The company has built its pipeline through acquisition and has been profitable since 2004. Again, the ability of the company to launch this public offering was a function of its uncharacteristically late stage of development.

Jennerex Biotherapeutics successfully raised $5.5 million in September for their targeted gene therapies for cancer. They are currently in Phase II for liver cancer and Phase I for several others. And, Endocyte closed a $26 million extension of its Series C offering in October to fund its multiple Phase II trials in cancer using their folate receptor drug guidance system and in molecular imaging for their companion diagnostic approach. In a follow-on financing Metabolon increased its Series C round to a total of $12.3 million to fuel progress in its metabolomics-driven biomarker discovery and analysis platform. Continuing the trickle of public offerings in the second half of the year, Talecris Biotherapeutics went public on the NASDAQ exchange in September, selling 44,736,842 shares at $19 per share and placing a further 6,000,000 in underwriters overallotment shares. 21,052,632 of the shares came from Cerberus Plasma Holdings LLC, which is managed by Cerberus Partners LP in a joint venture with Ampersand Ventures. This major liquidity event gave Cerberus a $1.9 billion, or 21-fold, partly realized gain on its original investment of $90 million. Including two cash dividends amounting to $833 million that investors received in 2005 and 2006 the joint venture posted a $2.6 billion in partly realized gain on their original joint investment of $125 million. Talecris Biotherapeutics now has a market capitalization of $2.7 billion. Talecris also launched a private offering immediately after the IPO to raise $600 million more in senior notes not due until 2016. The company used the proceeds of both transactions to pay down debt and free up their revolving credit line. Talecris is a well established plasma protein therapeutics company which the investors originally bought from Bayer AG as a distressed asset. Over the five years the investors worked with the company EBITDA (earnings before interest, taxes, depreciation, and amortization) rose from $65 million to $264 million and revenues rose to $1.1 billion from $864 million. Their gross profit margin also catapulted from 22% to 39%. Only a company with this sort of performance could have got out of the IPO gate just as it opened.

And the following month, another metabolomics company, Metabolex, raised a $8.6 million round for their first in class type 2 diabetes therapy, focused on G protein-coupled receptor 119, that had yielded positive results in two Phase I trials.

In November, BioVex, another oncolytic virus therapeutic company, expanded its F round of financing to a total of $70 million to fund its Phase III pivotal studies of oncolytic vaccines OncoV-EX^{GM-CSF} for head and neck cancer and OPTiM for Melanoma. The company is focused on oncology and infectious disease and is testing its anti-genital herpes treatment ImmunoVEX^{HSV2} in the United Kingdom. This raise was one of the largest for the year. Ironwood Pharmaceuticals filed its registration statement for an IPO this same month, although the offering bled into 2010 with the underwriters overallotment closing in February. Nevertheless, Ironwood raised a net of $203 million, leaving it with $302 million cash in hand for ongoing programs. The company is collaborating on Linaclotide with both Forest Labs and Astellas and had a positive Phase III report in early November for patients with chronic constipation. The company is also seeking to add to its pipeline for pain, inflammation, asthma and cardiovascular indications and now has the war chest to do so.

December was Zogenix's turn to raise a total of $71 million in a two-stage Series B round for their proprietary needle-free delivery system for drugs for central nervous system (CNS) disorders and pain. The company had its first drug approved in July for migraine and cluster headaches and is in late stage development of a second drug for pain.

At least two other companies filed registration statements for IPOs in the fourth quarter but, as of this writing, neither Tengion nor Trius Therapeutics had priced their offerings.

SO, WHAT ARE THE TAKE HOME MESSAGES OF THE PRIVATE DEAL FLOW OF 2009?

There were some favored therapeutic areas, such as oncology & oncolytic viruses, metabolomics, miRNA/RNAi, anti-infectives and antivirals. There were even some gene therapy and stem cell financings as well as some vaccine plays. But, what most companies that received financing had in common with each other was that they had some positive clinical data with at least something in Phase II and/or Phase III, and a pipeline behind those. They also frequently had secured orphan indication status for one or more of their candidates and had collaborations, partnerships or option agreements with big pharma and/or large biotech or investment from the venture arms of those organizations. Some came armed with management teams who were alums from other already successful big biotech ventures. As a result, many of these rounds of financing were quite large from $20 million A rounds to $46 million C rounds to $50 million F rounds.

Going into 2010, entrepreneurs seeking funding for their early stage ventures have to either have some of these characteristics in place or have a game plan for how the money they hope to raise will help them acquire these attractive profiles and secure these sorts of investments down the road. Even family, friends & fools, and especially angels, do not want to invest in a pier although they may go for a bridge to a professional round.

WHAT DOES THE PUBLIC MARKETPLACE PERFORMANCE MEAN TO ENTREPRENEURS?

While the public market began to show some signs of life in the second half of the year, the companies that were able to launch did so at a much later stage of development than historically has been necessary. As a result, they priced out at very respectable levels even if there was some last minute price retrenchment for some. The public market will need to be far more robust for companies without approved product on the market and a robust pipeline partnered with larger firms to succeed in getting out.

What is also important to the entrepreneur is how the companies who have managed to go public in more biotech-friendly environments are managing to keep their programs funded while the public marketplace is relatively tight. This is important, because when the public market is not available for secondary offerings, public companies turn to private equity deals to raise capital. Private equity investors find public companies more mature and less inherently risky (and more liquid) than earlier stage ventures, and money naturally migrates away from early stage investments. This phenomenon is arguably what has been fueling the increasingly deeper and wider 'valley of death' that small firms have to navigate.

So what did public biotechnology companies do to raise capital in 2009, and did it actually impact the availability of capital to fund private biotechnology companies? We will not do a detailed analysis of the deal flow in this case as it is more the volume of deals, the vehicles used to fund them and who was providing the capital that is relevant here.

The good news is that public biotechnology companies did manage to raise quite a lot of capital in 2009. The less good news is that there was a migration from classic secondary offerings, and even 144a offerings or PIPEs (private placements into public entities), in favor of the emergence of "modified dutch auction" tender offers, bought deal financings, and rights offerings or registered direct financing offerings as a preferred route for private capital to enter public companies. In part this is driven by the desire of public companies to avoid the inevitable arbitrage that often depresses their stock price in a classic offering. The popularity of 144as and PIPEs in prior years testifies to this since in both instances the pricing of the deal is far more insulated. However, the shares issued in those scenarios typically have liquidity restrictions requiring minimum holding periods before they can be sold in the open market. That feature has not been considered attractive in the very skittish marketplace of the last twelve months. Shares issued through Registered Direct Financing

Offerings in contrast provide the public company with the advantage of a managed offering at a managed price and the investor with shares that are immediately tradable—hence their rapid adoption and popularity. However, there was still some pain involved in securing these investments with many companies having to clear debt from their books, buy back existing warrants, or do a reverse stock split and restructure themselves before the investment was made. Moreover, these offerings often consisted of both stock and warrants thereby increasing the potential long term upside for the investor without all of the upfront risk.

On balance, firms managed to prosper in hard times and keep their programs moving along even if they have needed to trim their sails here and there. And, some of the public biotechs are getting large enough that they need to go shopping for pipeline among the earlier stage companies creating new opportunities for partnering. This is just as well, since the number of big pharma companies has been shrinking due to mergers and acquisitions. The beauty pageant is on.

REFERENCES

1. Report from the National Governor's Council: Experts' Roundtable on Angel Investing and State Policy Kansas City, Missouri, 2006
2. Stanford University School of Business
3. MoneyTree Report 2010—PriceWaterhouseCoopers & National Venture Capital Association available online at www.pwcmoneytree.com & www.nvca.org

CHAPTER **6**

Partnering With Industry

Bethany Mancilla, MBA
Vice President, Business Development and Licensing, PharmAthene, Inc.

The aim of this chapter is to provide the biotechnology entrepreneur with an overview of the rationale and process for establishing industry partnerships. The chapter focuses on creating an alliance with a pharmaceutical or biotechnology company for product development and progress toward the marketplace that would be more difficult without such a relationship. The topics covered, however, can be generally applied to diagnostic or service-based partnering opportunities. The chapter will explore the process of identifying, contacting, meeting, negotiating, completing, and maintaining an industry partnership.

INTRODUCTION

You cannot go it alone; it is too expensive, too long, and too complicated. Consequently, establishing partnerships with industry is often a prerequisite for survival and success of a biotechnology company. Start-up companies are not typically able to discover, develop and commercialize their own products from inception. Instead, companies evolve through a series of developmental milestones triggering opportunities for further growth and financing requirements. A key source for furthering that growth and funding is through industry partnerships. These partnerships have become particularly important for start-up companies as the level of available of venture capital (VC) funds are cyclical and unpredictable. Toward the end of the first decade of the new millennium, the majority of top-tier VC funds had less than 50% of their funds available[1], acquisitions of private companies were down 66% since 2007[2] and initial public offerings were shut-down in 2008.

Table 1 highlights some of the key reasons biotechnology companies pursue industry alliances. Whatever the reason, knowing what you are trying to achieve will help establish the structure and terms of your alliance. Deals can vary depending upon the amount of risk and reward you and your prospective partner are willing to agree upon ranging from a license with or without a collaboration, an option to license, a co-development partnership, a co-promote deal or a merger and acquisition (see Table 2).

Co-development and co-promotion deals typically occur when a biotechnology company has financial leverage and competing bidders, allowing the company to remain active in the development and commercialization of the product. The average start-up company is not in a financial position or at a point of clinical validation—proof-of-concept in a patient population—where these structures would likely be of interest to a prospective pharmaceutical company partner.

The more likely deal structure for a start-up company is a license or option-to-license. The option-to-license structure has increased substantially since 2005, with a nearly four-fold increase in the

Table 1: Reasons to partner

Reason	Start-up objectives
Financing	Obtain funding to support product development, manufacturing, and commercialization Sell equity to industry partner at a premium Further other public or private financing opportunities
Validate business	Confirm market interest in the opportunity Create commercial path for opportunity
Access resources	Share development activities Tap into specific manufacturing capabilities Access sales and marketing infrastructure
Access IP and know-how	Obtain intellectual property and know-how for freedom to operate or product commercialization

Table 2: Representative deal structures

	Option to license	License	Co-development	Co-promote
Product development & commercialization	Biotechnology company develops with funding from pharmaceutical company typically thru Phase II proof-of-concept when pharmaceutical company can exercise option. Pharmaceutical company completes development and commercialization.	Pharmaceutical company may develop product or fund biotechnology company to develop the product. Pharmaceutical company commercializes product.	Pharmaceutical company and biotechnology share in product development based on negotiated terms. Pharmaceutical company assumes commercialization unless there is agreement to co-promote.	Pharmaceutical company and biotechnology company share sales and marketing costs based upon harmonized marketing strategy.
Product risk	Biotechnology company has product risk until option exercised then pharmaceutical company assumes product development risk.	Pharmaceutical company assumes product development risk.	Pharmaceutical company and biotechnology company share product development risk based upon their contribution.	Pharmaceutical company and biotechnology company share sales and marketing risk.
Product value	Value to biotechnology company is capped upfront and contingent on milestones. Contingency payments take into account product development risk assumed by pharmaceutical company.	Value to biotechnology company is capped and committed to upfront and takes into account product development risk assumed by pharmaceutical company.	Pharmaceutical company and biotechnology company share in product value based upon their contribution to product development.	Pharmaceutical company and biotechnology company share in revenue streams based upon the contribution to sales and marketing.

number of deals done with pharmaceutical company and big biotechnology companies having this structure.[3] The option-to-license deal allows a pharmaceutical company to have guaranteed access to the program at capped prices if the program meets agreed upon milestones—but no long-term funding requirement if the program fails. In exchange, the biotechnology company receives funding that allows the company to support at least part of the development, increasing the likelihood of a deal with large pre-defined milestone payments based upon success. So long as the financial market favors the buyer, the option-to-license structure is likely to continue to grow.

The start-up can use that capital to promote itself and its technology. Your company will appear more attractive and less risky to investors and other potential licensees. It is not cliché that the first deal is the hardest one. Use the first one as a lure to attract others. Entrepreneurs should consider if there are different ways their inventions could reach the marketplace. For example, is there more than one disease indication for which it could be applied? If so, there is a potential licensee for each product reaching the market—even if it the same product. Just as a slice of cake at a restaurant costs more per piece than buying the whole thing, dividing one's technology into several licensing opportunities helps maximize returns and diversify development risk. Yes, it can be difficult to balance developing a diverse pipeline—but it is worth the effort.

IDENTIFYING PARTNERS

The set of prospective partners will clearly depend upon the opportunity being solicited and the objectives you are trying to achieve. If your partnering objective is driven by a need to obtain rights to intellectual property, then your partnering target may already be defined. But in the case where the drivers for partnering are to raise money, validate the business, or access resources, the list will be more extensive. The process for identifying prospective partners can be driven by evaluating companies from those different perspectives.

FINANCING DRIVER

Certainly, a major driver of most partnerships with industry is access to deeper pockets (addressed in *Resource Driver,* below). Pharmaceutical companies know what it takes to develop products and have the means to do it. However, what determines whether a pharmaceutical company is interested in partnering will depend upon how well the opportunity aligns with their priorities, and whether or not they view your company as a viable and stable solution to their needs. How you present and position your firm will go a long way to determining their level of interest.

How do you start assessing their needs, which must be done before even considering their level of interest?

Some of the needs of a company can be determined by just reading their press releases and annual reports. Often, the CEO will convey the strategic direction for the company and indicate whether certain areas are of higher or lower importance. A simple Internet search can sometimes provide links to presentations made by senior executives where relevant company information can be found. Corporate websites may also contain information on business development and licensing group activities and where specific areas of interest reside. Not surprising, this is often tied to specific therapeutic areas of interest, stages of development or product enabling platform capabilities.

Having knowledge of target company priorities allows you to look at how your opportunity aligns and could be of benefit to the prospective partner. Doing this homework prior to contacting a prospective partner helps you position your opportunity in a meaningful way. If your program does not fit with the priorities of the prospective partner, it does not mean there may not be interest. On the contrary, it just means that it will be a less intuitive alliance—and therefore a harder sell. Those potential partners may fall onto a "B" list which you still pursue, but understand it may be a longer "selling cycle" (the time from initial contact to final execution).

If you are interested in having a pharmaceutical company make an equity investment in your company as part of the partnership, then it is worth evaluating whether they have made such investments in the past and on what terms. For example, did they pay a premium price per share on equity they purchased and if so, what percentage premium did they pay? If they have not, you may want to find out what it would take for them to be receptive to the idea. Evaluating the structure of deals a prospective partner has made in the past is a helpful exercise in general particularly when it comes to developing a proposed deal structure. In your role of "corporate archeologist," the information sought may sometimes be publicly limited or unavailable. Under such circumstances—where websites and press releases provide inadequate insight—subscription sites can be useful (*e.g.*, Recap, MedTrack, LexusNexus, Frost and Sullivan, etc.).

VALIDATION DRIVER

The market tends to view a large pharmaceutical company partnership as a key validating step in a biotechnology company's evolution. Whether you validate the business with a top 5 pharmaceutical company partner or a top 50 pharmaceutical company, the success of your start-up will not depend on their marquee status. What you need to consider is the credibility of the pharmaceutical company—and if your shareholders and investors will view the partner as a long-term commercial player capable of supporting the ultimate commercial success of your product. Your target partnering list will be impacted by the importance of this objective—but may be secondary if financing dominates development of your prospective list.

RESOURCE DRIVER

Many early-stage companies are in the discovery or initial steps of pre-clinical/clinical development, and funding has not been used to establish manufacturing and commercialization infrastructure. Whereas, traditional pharmaceutical companies have a full spectrum of resources they can apply to a partnership including downstream manufacturing and sales and marketing capabilities.

If your opportunity will require a Food and Drug Administration (FDA)-approved manufacturing facility, it is worth considering whether the prospective partner has this capability in-house. Although, in recent years, pharmaceutical companies have been expanding their biologics pipeline[4], their manufacturing capabilities and capacity may not be sufficient to meet the demands of the partnership. It is worth knowing whether the target partner could provide this capability to the partnership.

The list of potential partners from the financing list will likely dictate which partners have an interest in a partnership. The intersection of this list with the list of target companies from your validation list will help establish a prioritized list of companies for you to pursue.

MAKING CONTACT

Once you have your list of target companies, you can determine whether you or individuals associated with your company have direct contacts. If not, there are different means of making contact such as networking at conferences or local events, sending a letter or email, or placing a direct call. These approaches are second nature for business development executives but may be new for a start-up or first-time entrepreneur. Just keep in mind that on the other end is another professional who is just trying to do their job. If your message resonates with their objectives either individually or as a company, they are more than likely going to want to learn more.

Initial contact can be made through business development or R&D. The person you approach does not have to be at the highest level in the company. In fact, going in at a senior level without a contact or credible introduction will not always get you through the door faster. Even if you do go through senior management contacts, deals typically progress down a due diligence and approval process defined by each company that involves key stakeholders in the decision—including mid-level and line management.

Having a board member or other affiliate of the company reach out through a relationship to a senior executive at the prospective company is a powerful way to get deal visibility and priority within the organization. Timing for leveraging that relationship is subjective, but using it once the company has expressed interest and the due diligence process has been initiated can help drive the deal to closure. Consideration should be taken in deploying this tactic as it can alienate your champion in the company rather than facilitate the process. If you know contact is going to be made at a level above your contact, you may want to inform your contact.

Who the champions, decision-makers, influencers and stake-holders are in the process is your job to uncover. Often, these individuals can be determined through conversations with your key point of contact. This knowledge is helpful because it will allow you to hone in on the questions, concerns and issues important to the people who will be driving the decision.

In particular, business partnering conferences are a good means for a company will little visibility to gain exposure to key executives and stake-holders. Although not inexpensive to attend, the primary purpose of such conferences is bringing together—face-to-face—two entities with common interests and alignments. Such conferences are in stark contrast to the technical/scientific bent of the meetings with which most entrepreneurs are more familiar. Think of them as the corporate partnership version of speed-dating. One-on-one meetings are requested by one party of another, after looking at all the profiles listed for the conference attendees. Such meetings are commonly 30 minutes, which means the entrepreneur must be clear and concise in their message—all the while leaving time for your "date" to tell theirs. The purpose of this whirlwind introduction is to generate sufficient interest for a follow-up get-together—either during the conference or afterwards. If a company accepts your meeting request, you already know they have at least a threshold level of interest in what you have to offer. Thus, you avoid the feeling of a "cold call" or half-hearted audience—and can immediately get down to business. Lastly, such partnering conferences are held in/with all major market regions, including Europe, India, Japan, and China.

COMMUNICATING

Delivering your message is where your homework comes into play. Tailoring your opportunity to align with the interest and needs of the prospective partner can make the opportunity more tangible and relevant to the prospective partner. Developing your value proposition will help the prospective partner sell the deal internally. The value proposition can apply to the product opportunity (*e.g.*, novel mechanism of action, patented field of interest) and, if possible, specifically to a prospective partner's need (*e.g.*, fill a pipeline gap, accelerate a strategic direction). Whatever your value proposition is, the more you can qualify and quantify it relative to your target audience's interest, the more you will help advance your discussions.

Listening is also an important element of deal making. One approach that can help get an opportunity aligned is to ask the prospective partner what it would take for them to get the deal done. If what you hear is within your ability to provide, either in the near to mid-term, you can begin to build a structure for the partnership that they will likely support.

The level of communication typically begins on a non-confidential basis and evolves based upon the degree of interest by the partner to a confidential basis. Many pharmaceutical companies do not like to enter into confidentiality agreements until they are sure they have an interest in a potential partnership. The process for getting a confidential disclosure agreement (CDA) in place can actually take time if the partner is worried about the risk of contaminating information being shared in an area of work where they have internal efforts underway. Until a CDA is signed, it can be a balancing act between how much you are willing to share to progress your discussions and what is risky based upon unprotected intellectual property, know-how and business strategy.

MEETINGS

Meetings are an integral step in the process of establishing a partnership; however, they consume resources on both sides of the table and can be unproductive and even fateful if not well planned. Key components for a successful meeting include having an agreed upon agenda covering topics of interest to the partner and having appropriate representatives from both companies at the meeting. Meetings can backfire when the focus goes outside areas of interest to the prospective partner. It is easy to get onto topics related to your program but not necessarily relevant to the prospective partner.

There is a balancing act between being interactive and responsive to questions the partner may ask and getting through all the topics the partner wants to cover. In a situation where you see the time getting off track, you can pause the meeting for a time check and just ask the partner what their preference is for prioritizing the remainder of the time. Facilitating a productive meeting is part of the biotechnology company's job.

DUE DILIGENCE

Assuming the prospective partner is interested in progressing potential partnering discussions following initial meetings, the next stage is the process of due diligence. Depending upon the stage of development of the program, the partner will want to review critical components of the program that confirm the validity of the opportunity.

The degree of information you can expect a prospective partner to want to review depends upon the stage of product development. For a start-up company that is earlier in development the list is usually shorter. Below is a list of due diligence materials that a partner may request.

Product information:
- Scientific background
- Efficacy data
- Safety data

Intellectual property/licenses:
- Copies of all patents and patent applications related to the product
- Copies of all licenses held related to the product
- Any IP work done on freedom to operate with respect to product

Business plan:
- Financial *pro forma*
- Development strategy
- Management backgrounds

Preclinical/clinical:
- Details of data produced by all preclinical/clinical trials

Regulatory:
- FDA meeting minutes
- Investigator Brochure
- Results of regulatory inspections

Manufacturing:
- Facility information
- Inspection summaries
- Process validation report
- Economics of manufacturing process

Quality:
- Current status of quality system implementation

The process of due diligence can be facilitated by centralizing this information prior to initiating partnering discussions. The information can be assembled in an electronic data room for simplicity and security, or bound and numbered for ease of reference. Whether electronically or on paper, you want to appear as sophisticated and organized as possible in order to continue the positive impression already in place. Without that initial positive impression, due diligence would not be underway in the first place. You would not necessarily trust a doctor who had trouble locating your medical information, or an accountant who put your tax return amongst a pile of documents on their desk. So, do not expect any less scrutiny from those conducting due diligence. Further, having your information in a clear, organized manner shows you care about the other party's time and interest. Certainly, streamlined due diligence is insufficient for the successful execution of a deal. However, given that the pharmaceutical or biotechnology partner likely has more suitors than deals, you want to do all you can to put your company at the top of their list.

Due diligence is an iterative process and can take several meetings and teleconferences to complete. The value of the deal will hinge upon the confirmation of data retrieved from this process. Since no pharmaceutical company executive wants to look foolish, they will make sure relevant stakeholders, influencers and decision-makers have evaluated the opportunity and that each of their concerns are adequately addressed. During this process, it is helpful to identify who the champion for the opportunity is and to work closely with them to help them sell the deal internally.

DEVELOPING AND NEGOTIATING THE TERM SHEET

In parallel with the due diligence process, it is helpful to establish a proposed deal structure prior to creating the term sheet. This can be a conceptual document that addresses at a high-level what the partnership will look like. For example, if there are multiple areas where the parties could collaborate, agreeing upon what those may be in advance of developing the term sheet will help guide the terms that get included in the term sheet.

There are a few key areas of importance that a typical term sheet includes the:

- Scope of the collaboration
- Definition of the product
- R&D program
- Intellectual property
- License grant
- Territory
- Financials

These components are interconnected and influence the financials. To establish the financial terms there are two principle methods currently used to value drug development opportunities[5]: risk adjusted net present values (rNPVs) and comparables. Having a couple of approaches for determining value allows the parties to triangulate particularly when there are value gaps in what each party is trying to achieve.

RNPVS

Risk adjusted NPVs take into account the forecasted revenue streams from the program, subtract the costs of development, then discount the remaining cash flows. Discounting the remaining cash flows takes into account both the capital asset pricing model discount (CAPM) and the technical risks associated with failure of the program based upon the different stages of development.[6] Below is a summary of industry risks and timelines associated with clinical development that get factored into rNPV models.[7,8]

Stage of development	Passing rate	Timeline for stage of development
Phase I	70%	1 year
Phase II	47%	2 years
Phase III	80%	3 years

NOTE: The passing rate is what percentage of compounds entering the stage of development will pass that stage. For phase I safety, 70% of the compounds entering that stage will pass and enter into stage II. Of compounds entering Phase II, 47% will pass and go on to phase III. Phase II is made up of IIa and IIb and therefore the 47% is a combination of the pass rates for IIa and IIb. Phase III is what percentage of compounds entering Phase III will pass Phase III.

The issue with early-stage programs is determining the forecasted sales when the product profile and indication space are not well known. The "valuation gap" refers to the difference between what a biotechnology company may believe those sales opportunities are and what a pharmaceutical company believes they are. Since a valuation gap can be significant, this is where contingency payments can be built into the proposed deal structure.

The value of a program that the biotechnology company retains depends upon the stage of development. The further developed the product and the less risk associated with the program, the more value the biotechnology company (licensor) will retain. The further the product is from market and the more risk associated with the program, the more value the pharmaceutical company (licensee) will retain. Below is a table outlining the value allocation a biotechnology company may expect based upon the stage of development of the program.[9,10]

Value distribution

Stage of development	Preclinical	Phase I	Phase II	Phase III	Pre-Market
Value to biotechnology company (licensor)	20-25%	30%	50%	60%	70%
Value to pharmaceutical company (licensee)	75-80%	70%	50%	40%	30%

Pre-market is the period following Phase III clinical trials when submission of the NDA/BLA to the FDA is underway and prior to FDA licensure of the drug or biologic. Although the risk is lower at this phase, there is still a risk and partnering will take that into account.

COMPARABLES

Having comparables for like types of deals can help close the value gap. When referring to comparables, remember factors that may have influenced the terms, such as ill-defined target populations at the time of the deal or lack of bargaining power. Direct comparables may not always be available—particularly if the product is novel. Still, you can be certain the pharmaceutical company is looking into them and will use them as a proxy for the terms they discuss with senior management.

Below is a table of average deal terms for compounds licensed by biotechnology companies to pharmaceutical companies between 2001-2006 based upon deals captured in the Recap Database (www.recap.com), and evaluated by Mark Edwards, President Deloitte Recap, and colleagues. These are average terms for compounds across a wide-range of therapeutic indications. They provide a ballpark estimate for the type of terms you might expect based upon the stage of your program.[11]

Reaching final terms is a process of give and take where factors such as the breadth of the license, number of disease indications, competing products and the territory can be used as building blocks to help you reach the value you are trying to achieve. During the negotiation process, be prepared with alternative scenarios you can "live with" that redistributes the payments by rebalancing upfront payments to later milestones and royalty while maintaining the overall value you are targeting. Ultimately, the value of the program

Vanilla terms for compound deals (2001-2006)

	Preclinical (near IND)	Phase I	Phase II (some human POC)	Phase III
Upfront	$3-10MM	$5-15MM	$10-25MM	$40-100MM
IND	$2-5MM	NA	NA	NA
Phase II start	$3-8MM	$5-10MM	NA	NA
Phase III start	$10MM	$10-15MM	$25MM	NA
NDA filing	$5MM	$5MM	$10MM	$30MM
1st approval	$5MM	$10MM	$30MM	$50MM
2nd-3rd approval	$10MM	$20MM	$45MM	$70MM
Royalty tiers	9-13%	12-15%	14-20%	18-26%

In license agreements there can be royalty stacking provisions to account for the potential of the licensee to have to pay multiple royalties for different rights needed to commercialize the product. For example, an agreement may propose that in the event a combined royalty burden for a product exceeds a defined percent, then the royalty payable to the licensor is proportionally adjusted based upon the percent contribution to the royalty burden. These provisions ensure that the licensee is not unwilling to commercialize the product due to the cumulative nature of royalty obligations and the economic attractiveness of the product compared to other product opportunities in the licensee's pipeline. To protect the originator from getting over-diluted, anti-stacking provisions limit the amount of reduction in royalty acceptable and establish a floor for the expected royalty rate.

is what the buyer is willing to pay.

Although the financials are a significant element of the deal negotiations, careful consideration should be given to the license grant and the rights the partner will receive. It is a worthwhile investment to have an experienced intellectual property attorney review the terms to ensure your intentions are appropriately reflected. The definitions that get translated into the actual agreement should reflect the intent of the terms you agreed upon in the term sheet, unless mutually agreed to otherwise. The term sheet can become a helpful reference when the negotiation of the agreement gets off-track.

FINALIZING THE DEAL

Once the key terms of the deal are within range for both parties, an agreement can be drafted. The deal is still in an active phase of negotiation and requires thoughtful consideration. It is good to be the originator of the draft agreement as it provides an opportunity to think through all the terms and draft them to be fair to your company. The more onerous and one-sided the terms are, the longer the negotiations will take, and the risk of creating ill-will in the relationship can occur. During the negotiations it is good to keep in mind that the partnership is not over when the deal is signed; in fact, it is just beginning. No deal can anticipate all future events, so creating a good working relationship, knowing you may have to address unexpected events and negotiate future amendments to the agreement, is advisable.

Undoubtedly, the degree of flexibility in the terms that can be negotiated with a pharmaceutical company partner will be based upon the degree of leverage you have in the process. It is beneficial to have at least one other party interested in the program so a floor in the negotiations can be established. Although confidentiality will certainly prevent you from telling Company B the details of a potential deal with Company A, being able to say you have a term sheet or draft term sheet ("bullet point") with an undisclosed entity will generate additional interest. Being able to say an undisclosed entity has entered into due diligence—while not as compelling—may generate additional interest if the process with Company A is not as far along. Continuing to build outside interest in your program—despite advanced discussions with a pharmaceutical company partner—is a challenge. However, continuing efforts with other parties is important not only because a deal is not done until it is done, but also because a pharmaceutical or biotechnology company knows when you are desperate.

In the process of negotiating, it is good to identify the terms that are key to you and the terms that you are willing to give on. You can use the "give-in" terms to help get you where you want to be with the key terms. Before a call to negotiate terms, it is worthwhile to think through the discussion and even role play with a colleague to anticipate the issues and comments you will need to overcome.

As you work through the agreement, be aware of the partner's approval process. Each company has its own process for approval. This process can become a gating factor in getting the deal signed—particularly if you miss a periodic review meeting that does not happen frequently but is required for final signature. Also, if you are planning to issue a press release announcing the deal, this will also require adequate review and time for approval by the pharmaceutical/biotechnology company. Whether a pharmaceutical company is prepared to review a press release or not is a good sign of where you are in the process. The partner may not want a press release in cases where: a) the deal is small and exploratory in scope, and/or b) it may wish to keep the project secret.

There is regular dialogue between the parties when a deal is in active negotiations. If days pass without discussion or advancement, there could be reason for concern. You should determine if something can be done to pro-actively address any issues your partner may be confronting based upon feedback they are receiving from their internal constituencies.

ALLIANCE MANAGEMENT

Once a deal is finalized, the work actually begins and the process outlined by the agreement takes effect. The governance of the program depends upon the nature of the deal but is usually overseen by a joint steering committee. The steering committee meets on a regular basis (*e.g.*, quarterly) to discuss the progress of the program and address any issues that may need to be resolved. Having individuals on the steering committee who were involved in establishing the partnership provides continuity and is helpful when questions arise regarding the intent of the program.

The relationship between the parties is important and will set the tone for whether or not there will be a willingness to expand the partnership based upon options in the agreement or if new opportunities develop. To ensure the partnership is successful, it is good to have an internal program management function tracking progress and driving the program on a day-to-day basis.

When issues arise, the best approach is a thoughtful, pro-active approach. Identify both the issue as well as potential solutions, and provide a recommendation for the partner to consider. If the issue is critical to the program, it may require meeting outside of the planned steering committee meeting. The credibility of your company will be influenced by how difficult issues are handled—and undoubtedly they will happen. Establishing a communication plan to deal with these obstacles will ensure your team is on the same page with regards to the plan and your message is consistent.

Getting successfully through your first issue is a sign of strength in your relationship. If the relationship is strained, the alliance management function may need to compensate and take extra steps to smooth it out. This may include a special face-to-face meeting either in a formal or informal setting to talk through the issues and reassure the partner of your company's intent. Just ignoring the issue will not make it go away.

In the end, the agreement is only a component of the partnership—and the relationship will determine whether the program is a success.

CONCLUSIONS AND TAKE-AWAYS

Completing a deal with a pharmaceutical/biotechnology company can take up to one year, and sometimes more, depending upon its complexity. Understanding the needs of your partner, and how they decide upon a deal, allows you to facilitate the process and pro-actively prepare for each step. The process of partnering with industry is a mix of art and science. Some of the do's and don'ts in the process are noted below:

Do
- Be prepared
- Articulate value proposition
- Have proof-of-concept
- Differentiate from competition
- Understand customer
- Be creative and flexible
- Build a relationship
- Listen
- Define a process

Don't
- Get off topic
- Give away your technology
- Assume you have no competitors
- Be unrealistic
- Be afraid to ask
- Give-up

Partnerships with industry are essential to financing life science product development. Making the partnership successful and producing a valuable new treatment is the ultimate goal, and requires a thoughtful agreement and strong relationship.

ACKNOWLEDGEMENTS:

I would like to acknowledge the valuable insights and recommendations regarding the content I have included in this chapter provided by Beth Burnside, PhD, Senior Vice President, Regulatory Affairs, Compliance & Strategic Planning, Middlebrook Pharmaceuticals, Inc., and Deborah Day Barbara, Vice President, Business Development, Strategic Diagnostics, Inc.

REFERENCES

1. Longman, R. (2009) Deal Making When Pharma's the Only Game in Town. Presented at the Pharmaceutical Strategic Alliances Conference; 23 September, New York City, New York

2. Longman, R. (2009) Secondary Directs: Tonic for the Biotech Venture Financing Model. Start-Up Emerging Medical Ventures 14 (8):14-17

3. Longman, R., Morrison, C. (2009) Deal Making When Pharma's the Only Game in Town. IN VIVO: The Business & Medicine Report 27 (8): 46-54

4. Lead Discovery. (2006) Big Pharma' Turns to Biologics for Growth to 2010: Segmentation by Drug Technology. Lead Discovery Publication, 4 May, http://leaddiscovery.co.uk/reports/376, Accessed 30 October 2009

5. Puran, S. (2009) The Valuation of Drug Development Projects—Part 1. Les Nouvelles, Journal of the Licensing Executives Society International 44 (3):180-188.

6. Bogdan, B., Villiger R. (2008) Basics of Valuation. In: Valuation in Life Sciences A Practical Guide. Springer: pp 45-48

7. DiMasi, J., Hansen, R., Grabowski, H. (2003) The Price of Innovation: New Estimates of Drug Development. Journal of Health Economics. 22:151-185

8. PhRMA. (2007) Drug Discovery and Development Understanding the R&D Process. PhRMA Publication, February, http://www.phrma.org/files/RD%20Borchure%20022307.pdf, Accessed 30 October 2009

9. Martin M. (2009) Negotiating Pharmaceutical Licensing Deal Structures: Confrontation or Common Ground?. Les Nouvelles, Journal of the Licensing Executives Society International 44 (3): 205-207

10. Avance. (2007) Discovery & Preclinical License Deals: What's Realistic? News in Avance, Valuation in Life Sciences, December, http://www.avance.ch/newsletter.docs/avance_on_deals.pdf, Accessed 30 October 2009

11. Edwards, M. (2007) Alliance Pricing Too Much of a Good Thing. Presented at the Allicense Conference; 11 April, San Francisco, California

CHAPTER 7

Licensing and Technology Transfer

Steven M. Ferguson, CLP
Deputy Director, Licensing & Entrepreneurship
Office of Technology Transfer, National Institutes of Health

Ruchika Nijhara, PhD, MBA
Senior Licensing Manager
Office of Technology Commercialization, Georgetown University

ABSTRACT

Over the past several decades, research conducted at university and federal laboratories has become more recognized as a potent resource for new and established companies. Such research is providing a wide range of benefits—ranging from inventions that are the basis of many new and improved products to access to human capital in terms of students, graduates, and faculty with specialized technical knowledge. Frequently, these new inventions and specialized technical knowledge can be combined with business and capital resources to be the basis of new, paradigm-shifting companies. In any case, the early developmental stage of innovations from these research programs—along with their institutional goals of providing access to the technology by the general public—make these research programs natural allies for bioentrepreneurs seeking new partners and technologies for early developmental stage companies.

INTRODUCTION TO U.S. BIOMEDICAL RESEARCH

For many years, the United States led the world in government support for non-military research and development (R&D), especially support for work that directly relates to health and human development. A focal point for such investments in biomedical research has been the National Institutes of Health (NIH), along with other federal laboratories and university-based research programs. Base funding (excluding economic stimulus funding) provided by the NIH alone reached $30.6 billion in fiscal year 2009 with approximately 10% of this funding spent on internal NIH R&D projects (intramural research) utilizing the work of about 6,000 scientists. The balance was used to support the work of 325,000 non-government scientists (extramural research) at 3,000 various colleges, universities and research organizations—such as Georgetown University—throughout the world.[1] Each year, this biomedical research leads to a large variety of novel basic and clinical research discoveries—all of which generally require commercial partners in order to develop them into products for hospital, physician or patient use. Thus, federal laboratories and universities need and actively seek corporate partners or licensees to commercialize its funded research into products in order to help fulfill their fundamental missions in healthcare, medical education and training.

WHY UNIVERSITIES AND FEDERAL LABS NEED BIOENTREPRENEURS

Licensing and technology transfer programs at non-profit basic research organizations provide a means for getting new inventions to the market for public use and benefit. From a research institution's perspective, this is quite desirable since with this public and commercial use of inventions would typically come with new recognition of the value of basic research programs at the university or organization that originated it. These inventions also serve as a helpful means to attract new R&D resources and partnerships to the laboratory.

Thus, through licensing or other technology transfer means there is also a "return on investment," whether that is measured in terms of financial, educational or societal parameters, or some combination thereof.

Because a substantial portion of the inventions that occur at basic research programs arise from research that is federally funded, there are also substantial legal requirements to promote commercial development of such new inventions. The Bayh-Dole Act of 1980 (P.L. 96-517) allows such grantees and contractors to seek patent protection on subject inventions made using federal funds, and to license those inventions with the goal of promoting their utilization, commercialization, and public availability. In 1986, federal laboratories were also given a statutory mandate under the Federal Technology Transfer Act (P.L. 99-502) and Executive Order 12591 to ensure that new technologies developed in federal laboratories were transferred to the private sector and commercialized.

Commercialization of inventions from non-profit basic research institutions typically follows a multi-step process, as academic and federal laboratories usually do not provide technology commercialization themselves. Technology commercialization is not a mission of such entities, and the resulting lack of necessary resources equates to much of the entrepreneurship in business arenas both within and outside of the life sciences. To begin the progression of a technology beyond the research institution, a contractual agreement (typically a license) is provided to give permission to use patents, materials, or assets to bring a product concept to market. Financial consideration or other benefits are received by the research institution in exchange through what is often an agreement with a small company who will bring in a large corporate partner later in development.

Since the 1980s, many federal labs and universities have developed a strategic focus for their technology transfer activities and are particularly interested in working with bioentrepreneurs. This is because revenue enhancement from licensing is no longer the sole institutional goal. Instead, these institutions find themselves also looking to increase new company formation based upon academic inventiveness, supporting faculty recruitment and retention, enhancing research funding, creating an entrepreneurial culture, attracting venture investment to their regions, and the like. The economic development aspects of research are being recognized as a fourth mission for such institutions—going along with education, research and public service. It is with this "fourth mission" that bio-entrepreneurs can play a key role in establishing or working with companies driven by new research discoveries. At the most enterprising and forward-thinking institutions, accomplishments factoring into the tenure process have expanded to include patents, industry board positions, and commercial activities (within ethical boundaries, of course). No longer are published papers, grant funding, and the number of mentored students the sole or predominant contributors to tenure decisions. Not surprisingly, when scientists and medical researchers are incentivized in entrepreneurial ways, entrepreneurship and company formation is fostered. Regions where such thinking is encouraged and supported are more often than not biotechnology hubs—Boston, San Francisco, etc.

SOURCES AND CHARACTERISTICS OF TRANSFERABLE TECHNOLOGY

Generally, bioentrepreneurs can directly access research and inventions for product development from three main sources. For research funded by grants and contracts from NIH or other federal agencies (extramural research), the individual university or small business grantees themselves would control commercial rights—with only standard obligations such as reporting and utilization obligations to the federal funding agency. This incentivized approach, which dates from the Bayh-Dole Act of 1980, has been attributed to the annual formation of nearly two new products and more than one new company each day, created through university technology transfer.[2] Biomedical research conducted directly by the federal laboratory (intramural research) is licensed directly through the affiliate technology transfer office.

Each of these institutions owns a robust research program "pipeline" that provides novel, fundamental research discoveries available for commercial applications. NIH, for instance, as both a large-scale provider and consumer, represents a sort of "supermarket" of research products and tools for its commercial partners and suppliers. Additionally, overall product sales of all types by NIH licensees exceed $5 billion annually. As previously mentioned, most technology transfer activities at NIH and other federal laboratories date from the Federal Technology Transfer Act of 1986. This legislation authorized formal research partnerships with industry. Also, it provided incentives to these programs to license technology by allowing the federal laboratory, for the first time, to keep its license royalties and share them between the individual inventors and their laboratories or institutes.

Research collaborations or assistance by federal laboratories and universities can take several forms. Perhaps the most common is the exchange of research materials through Material Transfer Agreements (MTAs). Recent efforts by the NIH have facilitated the rapid exchanges of such materials to and from NIH funded research programs using Simple Letter Agreements under the published NIH Research Tool Guidelines. Joint research projects are particularly important for bioentrepreneurs for basic research or clinical studies, called Cooperative Research and Development Agreements (CRADAs; at federal laboratories) or Sponsored Research Agreements (at universities) that grant desired license options to new discoveries. Because of their clinical hospitals and centers, as well as other networks and facilities, the NIH and at least some universities are able to take some of their medical discoveries (or those of their partners) into clinical trials through Clinical Trial Agreements. Basic research assistance may also be available to bioentrepreneurs through specialized services such as drug discovery, drug candidate compound screening, or testing services, offered by several programs or scientific training and exchange programs for individual investigators.

CHANGING LICENSING PRACTICES FAVOR STARTUPS AND SMALL BIOTECHNOLOGY FIRMS

The licensing practices for most non-profit research institutions—including federal institutions and universities—have changed significantly over recent years with respect to biomedical inventions.[3] With their ever-increasing consolidation, large pharmaceutical firms are typically no longer looking to directly license early-stage technologies for commercialization, and the number of licenses signed with startups as well as small to medium-sized biotechnology companies is on the rise. Unlike 10-15 years ago, when all or most of the high revenue medical products based on licenses from university or federal laboratory research came from large pharmaceutical firms, a majority of the latest success stories tend to be from biotech or other non-pharma companies. Some examples from the NIH licensing program are Kepivance® from Amgen, Velcade® from Millennium, Synagis® from Medimmune, and Taxus Express® from Angiotech. Although these are now all substantive, well-known companies, at the time the underlying technology was licensed to them they were not. The new reality is that commercial partners, especially small, innovative ones, are essential to the goals of biomedical research institutions seeing the results of their research become novel healthcare products for the public. Another reason that university licensing offices prefer licenses to a start-up company is because, unlike big companies, survival of the start-up company is dependent upon the development of the technology. Though they may have multiple products under development, most early-stage companies live or die based upon their lead program—for it is that lead program that investors are betting on. Start-up companies are highly motivated to successfully and expeditiously commercialize the licensed technology and expend all their resources toward its development. Most often, this option is better than licensing the technology to a big pharma or biotech company, where several technologies are being developed concomitantly. As a result, it is more likely that the university or federal research institution's technology may get scuttled ("put on the shelf") or de-emphasized if the risk profile becomes too high relative to other programs. However, the biggest challenge in licensing the technology to a start-up company is its chronically tenuous financial position; i.e., whether or not it can secure future capital to develop the technology in a timely fashion. Therefore, it is important that bioentrepreneurs have the drive and talent to do the right thing in the right way at the right time.

BASIC LICENSING PRINCIPLES FOR UNIVERSITY AND FEDERAL LABORATORIES

Compared to biomedical licensing from corporations, the federal laboratories and universities have a different focus and perspective when negotiating technology transfer agreements. Because these agreements are used to further overall institutional missions, representatives from such non-profit institutions consider the public consequences of such licenses as their first priority—not the financial terms that may be involved.

For example, compared with their peers in industry, non-profit institutions have the mandate to make technology as broadly available as possible. Thus, a strong preference exists to limit to the scope of a particular license to that needed to develop specific products. Exclusive licenses are quite typical for biomedical products such as vaccines and other medical therapeutics—where the underlying technologies require substantial private risk and investment (and a prior public notice and comment period in the Federal Register, in the case of federal laboratories). In their agreements, federal laboratories and universities also typically expect to retain the right to permit further research use of the technology to be conducted either in the intramural program, in universities, or in companies. Because the commercial rights granted represent institutional (and often public) assets, these agreements have enforceable performance benchmarks to ensure that the public will eventually receive the benefit (through commercialized products) of the research. Regulations governing the license negotiation of federally-owned technologies and their mandated requirements are described in more detail at 37 Code of Federal Regulations (CFR), Part 404, while those for federally-funded technologies can be found at 37 CFR, Part 401.

TYPES OF LICENSE AGREEMENTS

Universities and federal research institutions negotiate a variety of different types of license agreements for use and development of biomedical technologies. Besides offering exclusive and non-exclusive commercialization agreements for patented technologies, commercialization agreements are negotiated for unpatented biological materials. As a result of an increasingly selective patent strategy, both types of institutions do not try to patent technologies (*e.g.*, research materials or research methodologies) easily transferred for commercial use by biological material license agreements or publication. For patent rights or materials that are not to be sold as commercial products—but useful in internal R&D programs—both federal research institutions and universities typically negotiate non-exclusive, internal-use license agreements. Additionally, companies may obtain evaluation agreements to new technologies as well as specialized agreements relating to interference or other patent dispute settlements. Finally, for bioentrepreneurs interested in a technology that was jointly invented by two or more institutions, an inter-institutional patent/licensing management agreement would be negotiated. As a result, the bioentrepreneur would be able to obtain an exclusive license by dealing with only one party.

ROYALTIES AND ROYALTY NEGOTIATIONS IN LICENSE AGREEMENTS

Royalty rate negotiations with these institutions are influenced by factors commonly encountered in other negotiations of early-stage biomedical technologies (Table 1). Beyond these, there are negotiating factors unique to federal laboratories and universities, relating to the public health interest regarding the technology being licensed and the products to be developed from it (so-called "white knight clauses"). Examples of this may include: 1) supply back of materials for clinical use, 2) indigent patient access programs in the U.S., 3) commercial benefit sharing for natural product source countries, or 4) incentives for developing world access to the licensed products.

The royalty payments themselves consist of license payments received for execution royalties, minimum annual royalties (received regardless of the amount of product sales), earned royalties (a percentage of product sales), benchmark royalties, and payments for patent costs (Table 2). To date, due to conflict of interest concerns, the NIH has not sought equity payments in licenses or directly participated in company start-ups. Instead of equity, the NIH

Table 1: Factors influencing royalty rate negotiations with research Institutions

• Stage of development
• Type of product
• Market value of product
• Uniqueness of biological materials
• Scope of patent coverage
• Research institution "content"
• Public health significance

Table 2: Typical types of royalties in licenses agreements with research institutions

• Execution royalty
• Minimum annual royalty (regardless of the amount of net sales)
• Earned royalties (fixed % of net sales)
• Benchmark royalties
• Patent costs
• Equity (varies by institution)

can consider equity-like benchmark royalties that track commercial events at the company. However, many universities do take equity payments in their license agreements as a way to assist a new start-up company—despite the risk inherent in accepting equity in lieu of cash payments. The risk is considerable because such equity is illiquid, and has no present value at the time license is executed.

For several reasons, licensing institutions will often opt to take an equity or equity-like position when available from their licensees. For example, equity would provide for additional revenue in addition to the licensing royalties, especially if the licensed product failed in development but the company itself nevertheless becomes successful. Equity also can be seen as a risk premium for the research institution that provides additional inducement to grant the license to a new startup company verses a more established firm. Importantly (and perhaps most important for bioentrepreneurs), equity allows an licensee who is cash-poor but equity-rich to substitute an ownership position for a cash payment (in full or in part) for an upfront licensing fee and/or a reduced royalty rate. Finally, universities accept this risk to support their mission to assist in commercialization of early-stage technologies which may not be turned into marketable products otherwise, as well as encourage small business development. However, universities recognize that holding ownership rights in a start-up company creates potential conflict of interest, and so adopt various internal policies that mitigate and/or manage such conflicts.

Unlike their corporate counterparts, inventors at non-profit research institutions do receive a share of the royalties received from the licensing of their inventions. However each institution might have a slightly different revenue-sharing policy with respect to the percentage of licensing revenues provided to inventors. It is not surprising that those institutions offering inventors more lucrative terms are generally more active in licensing and commercialization. More recently, those institutions incentivizing their researchers—e.g., by having patents or patent applications factor in the tenure process—are also vibrant players in the world of bioentrepreneurs.

CHARACTERISTICS OF TYPICAL LICENSE AGREEMENTS

When licensing from a research institution, it is generally considered good business practices for the organization to standardize license terms to the greatest extent possible. Standardizing non-financial license terms levels the playing field for licensees—an important concept for public institutions—and creates a common understanding of the balance of risks acceptable to a research institution (which may differ markedly from the for-profit sector).

Given this drive for standardization, what might be some of the typical license agreements that a bioentrepreneur would come across in dealings with a non-profit research institution? Typically, federal research institutions and many universities have the types of license agreements shown in Table 3, and described below:[4]

Commercial evaluation license agreements are a short-term, non-exclusive license agreement allowing a licensee to conduct feasibility testing—but not sale of products developed from that technology. These typically run no longer than a few months, have a modest cost associated with them and include relevant materials that are supplied by inventor(s). Screening use is not permitted but the agreement has proven to be ideal for feasibility testing of new technologies

Table 3: Important types of license agreements involving research institutions

- Commercial evaluation / option license agreement
- Internal commercial use license agreement
- Research products commercialization license agreement
- Vaccine, diagnostic, therapeutic, or medical device product commercialization license agreement
- Inter-institutional agreements

that have a wide-variety of possible useful (but unproven) applications. Screening use implies use of the licensed material in the discovery or development of final end product. For example, a reporter cell that expresses a tumor target can be tested to screen drug candidates that could potentially be effective breast cancer therapeutics. Some universities may also use this type of agreement as a short-term exclusive option agreement for a nascent technology with the hope that a long-term diagnostic, vaccine or therapeutic product commercialization license agreement will later be completed.

Internal commercial use license agreements are another non-exclusive license agreement to allow a licensee to use (but not sell) technology in its internal programs. Here materials (either patented or unpatented) are provided, but screening uses are permitted. The financial structure of this agreement can be either a paid-up term license or annual royalty payments each, however, without any "reach through" royalty obligations to other products being used or discovered by the licensee. A paid-up term license would be a license in which the company makes one-time lump sum payment to obtain the rights to use the licensed technology for the duration of the license. On the other hand, "reach through" royalty provisions in a license agreement create royalties to the licensor on the future sales of downstream products that are discovered or developed through the use of licensed technology, even though the final end product may not contain the licensed technology. In other words, reach through royalties are royalties that are due to a licensor even though manufacture, use, sale of the final product does not infringe any patents claiming the licensed technology. Internal commercial use agreements themselves historically have been very popular with larger biomedical firms who are eager to acquire reagents to speed their internal development programs. Popular research products licensed in this manner include animal models and receptors.

Research products commercialization license agreements are also non-exclusive, but permit sales by the licensee to the research products market. Once more, materials (either patented or unpatented) are generally provided, with smaller firms predominating as licensees. For federal laboratories, U.S. manufacturing is required even for non-exclusive product sales in the U.S.—unless a waiver is granted. Such waivers are granted on the basis of lack of manufacturing capacity in the U.S. or economic hardship for the licensee. On the positive side, the financial structure of these licenses generally involves low upfront royalties. On the negative side, there are relatively high earned royalty payments since the materials provided are frequently close or very close to the finished product that is to be sold. Popular research products licensed in this manner include a wide variety of monoclonal/polyclonal antibodies or other research materials in basic studies.

Vaccine, diagnostic, therapeutic, or medical device product commercialization license agreements can be exclusive if such is necessary for product development. The exclusivity option is provided due to the capital and risk involved for the licensee. It is important for bioentrepreneurs to be aware that, by law, "small, capable" biomedical firms receive preference from federal laboratories and federally-funded universities as exclusive licensees. At NIH and other federal laboratories, all prospective grantees of exclusive licenses (identifying the licensee and technology by name) are published in the Federal Register for public comment or objections. A detailed development plan with product benchmarks or milestones is expected for licenses in this area. Collaborative research with federal laboratories regarding further pre-clinical or clinical development of the technology is encouraged—but not required—to obtain a license, and is negotiated separately by the individual laboratory. Moreover, these agreements have a requirement for U.S. manufacturing for U.S. product sales, unless a waiver is granted. The federal laboratory can typically grant waivers only when U.S. manufacturing sites are unavailable or manufacturing in the U.S. is economically unfeasible.

The financial structure of these licenses can involve substantial upfront royalties. However, they present much more moderate earned royalties and benchmark payments than those costing the entrepreneur less at the onset, since the technology is typically not as close to a completed, commercialized product. Other provisions to be negotiated include: 1) a share amount of sublicensing proceeds, 2) any of the public health "white knight" provisions described earlier, 3) licensee performance monitoring, and 4) audit requirements.

Inter-institutional agreements are often useful for exclusive licensing, as many commercializable technologies will often have inventors from more than one university or federal laboratory due to the collaborative nature of science. If a bioentrepreneur is seeking to obtain an exclusive commercialization license to increase investment interest and decrease risk, it is important to obtain the rights from all of the institutions involved—especially for U.S. patent rights—as all owners have the ability to license separately. Often, the joint owners of a single technology will pool their rights with a single party for patent and licensing purposes through an inter-institutional agreement. Such agreements provide significant convenience and time-saving for bioentrepreneurs, as negotiations with only a single party are necessary to provide the sought-after exclusive license.

ADVANTAGES OF WORKING WITH FEDERAL LABORATORIES AND UNIVERSITIES

Within these basic licensing structures, there are several advantages bioentrepreneurs can utilize in their product development efforts. Federal laboratories and universities offer favorable treatment to small businesses, and can create an attractive playing field for moving into new areas of product development.

For example, startups can utilize the expertise of the patent law firm hired by the institution to manage the prosecution of licensed technology. This is particularly useful for small firms that may not yet have internal patent counsel or the resources to retain a top—and thus usually expensive—intellectual property (IP) law firm.

Another useful distinction of license agreements with federal laboratories and universities—in contrast with corporate license agreements—is that they do not require bioentrepreneurs to cross-license existing rights they may own, give up any product marketing rights, nor forsake any downstream developmental rights. Also, research tool licenses negotiated through the NIH and many universities carry no grant-back or reach-through rights. For instance, when a research tool technology is licensed to a company by NIH, the licensee is not required to grant back any usage rights to the improvements that it may develop subsequent to the license agreement. Also, the licensee is not required to share with NIH any future profits that may be made as a result of improvements to the original discovery. In other words, IP derived from new discoveries made with NIH-licensed tools will remain clear and unencumbered.

Another advantage for a bioentrepreneur to license a technology from a non-profit institution is the flexibility in the financial terms. For example, reimbursement of back patent expenses, which the licensee typically pays upon the signing of the license agreement, could be deferred for a certain period of time. Similarly, the license deal could be structured to be heavily back-end loaded and/or equity-based, allowing the bioentrepreneur to apply its cash toward R&D. Unlike many research institutions that take equity in lieu of cash, federal institutions and some universities do not consider equity-based license deals. However, federal laboratories do consider taking equity-like benchmark payments via license deals. This lack of dilution may become an important feature as the bioentrepreneur looks to raise capital through each round of financing.

A bioentrepreneur could also take advantage of the capabilities and technical expertise residing in the licensor's laboratories by collaboration and/or sponsorship of the research needed to expedite the development the technology. While sponsoring research at the inventor's laboratory may raise conflict of interest issues, many institutions are willing to develop a conflict management plan with the engaged parties to help the start up exploit all the resources offered by the licensor. Nonetheless, many research institutions require execution of an agreement, separate from a license agreement, to formalize this arrangement.

ADDITIONAL CHARACTERISTICS OF AGREEMENTS WITH STARTUPS

Start-ups have the potential to produce significant opportunities for inventors, investors, research institutions, and regional economies. Still, such projects involve more work and are riskier than a traditional license to an existing, well-capitalized company. Although research conducted at federal laboratories and universities is not specifically designed to lead to new company formation, such activities are a way for such institutions to support the economic development aspects of their licensing and technology transfer programs. Successful start-up companies and bioentrepreneurs are highly prized because of the direct benefits to the community, region, state, and country in terms of new employment and tax revenue. Because of this, some research institutions have in-house business development staff dedicated to working with inventors as they consider startup opportunities for their technology. However, many institutions handle entrepreneurial activities of their researchers as part of the regular activities of the technology transfer office. Specialized staff members at the research institution are ideal contact points at institutions for bioentrepreneurs interested in company formation from a spin-out technology. They should be able to provide general assistance provide assistance in a number of activities including:

- Business planning
- Market analysis
- Identification of venture financing or other investments
- Regulatory planning
- Management
- Recruiting
- Miscellaneous business formation activities

A typical protocol for a research institution licensing to a start-up company is to first confirm that there is no other prior claim of rights from a commercial sponsor. Then, execute a letter of intent or other indication of interest, followed quickly with an option agreement to a future exclusive license. If the bioentrepreneur already has substantial resources in place, it may be possible to grant the license directly, in place of an option, when it is merited. Whatever the nature of the agreement, it is generally expected that the negotiation be with an officer of the new venture (or their attorney) rather than with a faculty member who may hope to be involved in the company. Agreements also would contain clear timelines to enforce diligent development of the technology toward commercialization. Deadlines are particularly critical for raising pre-determined levels of initial funding to establish and operate the venture. To avoid conflict of interest problems at the research institution, the new company would operate separately from the faculty inventor's lab—with local incubator or business park space being common options. Further, most research institutions would not allow their faculty inventors to serve as officers for the company without a leave of absence—but would allow these companies to collaborate and/or sponsor ongoing research in the laboratories of inventors subject to conflict of interest review and approval. Generally, a federal laboratory inventor is not able to have an active role in the company without leaving federal employment. The equity shares held by the research institution in these circumstances can vary by type of technology.

The actual equity share held by the research institution is often not that critical. The overall goal for the university or federal laboratory is to develop a robust local or regional corporate research community that closely complements and interacts with ongoing research at the institution. In addition, it is a way to support university or former federal faculty members who themselves are entrepreneurial and willing to commit their time and, often, their own money, to bringing their inventions to the marketplace.

ASSISTANCE PROGRAMS FROM UNIVERSITY AND FEDERAL LABS FOR STARTUPS AND BIOENTREPRENEURS

At a basic level, the success of a new biotechnology venture depends on five key ingredients: 1) technical expertise, 2) intellectual property assets, 3) business expertise, 4) physical space, and 5) money.[5] Institutional scientists or faculty entrepreneurs can provide the needed technical expertise (especially if students or post-docs can be hired by the new venture), and the research institutions themselves can license key patent rights to the company. But business expertise, space, and money are often more difficult to come by. Research institutions often try to bridge this gap by providing more than just IP licensing and technical expertise.

To address such needs, many research institutions have set up subsidiary organizations or utilize other academic departments at the university to help provide these types of dedicated services. Such services are often beyond the traditional scope and function of research and research administration at these institutions. For example, many university technology transfer offices also provide business and legal assistance to the start-up by collaborating with business and law schools at the university. Depending on the level of assistance needed and on the specifics of a particular program, the company can provide compensation for such assistance to the university through founder's equity. This equity is held by the university and transferred to business and finance office or investment office at the university which manages such equity until liquidation. In some instances, the assistance can go beyond that offered by in-house university business and law departments. One example is Spinner Technologies, Inc. created by the University of Virginia Patent Foundation in 2000. Spinner provides early-stage business expertise to faculty entrepreneurs and helps them find business partners to provide that expertise over the long run. Spinner also has a limited amount of wet lab space that it leases to faculty startups.[6] Other major universities such as the University of Utah, Columbia University, University of California at San Diego, and others, have been active in setting up such assistance programs, often in conjunction with university research parks, entrepreneurship centers or other affiliated facilities.[7]

Not surprisingly, obtaining seed-stage funding continues to be a significant problem for bioentrepreneurs—whether working with a faculty start-up or other early-stage company. To address this, groups at research institutions look to form a member-managed angel investment group—typically with a regional or alumni-based membership. The concept is for a group of individual angel investors to contribute to a pooled fund. Subsequently, they work together to evaluate companies affiliated in some manner with research institutions, deciding where and how much to invest. Many larger universities have, or are considering, such programs in conjunction with their technology transfer and university development offices. Some more established programs can be found at University of Florida, Marquette University, George Washington University, Illinois Institute of Technology, and others.[8] It is difficult to predict how well this model will work over time. Still, it is considered a potential means to fund early stage companies commercializing technologies licensed from university and federal labs, prior to their maturing into projects appropriate for investment. This method of support can work in concert with traditional federal funding sources, such as SBIR (Small Business Innovation Research) programs, STTR (Small Business Technology Transfer Research) programs,[9] and various state grants and loan programs

VALUE OF TECHNOLOGY TRANSFER AND LICENSING FROM UNIVERSITIES AND FEDERAL LABORATORIES

With their leading edge research programs and focus in the health-care market, federal laboratory and university-based research have an exemplary record in providing opportunities for bioentrepreneurs developing high growth companies and high growth medical products. Indeed, a preliminary study from 2007 showed that more than 100 drug and vaccine products approved by the U.S. FDA were based, at least in part, on technologies directly licensed from university and federal laboratories—with nearly 20% provided by federal labs (*e.g.*, NIH).[10] A subsequent study from 2009 showed that: 1) university-licensed products commercialized by industry created more than 279,000 jobs across the U.S. during a 12-year period, and 2) there was a increasing share of the U.S. gross domestic product each year attributable to university-licensed products.[11] This is an indication that the licensing of university and, by extension, federal laboratories, will have an increasingly effective and important impact well into the future.

This commercial success has been a model in demonstrating the value of technology transfer from federal laboratories, universities, and similar non-profit research institutions, but it is far from the entire story. The final tally must include the full societal value and economic impact of life-saving or enhancing therapeutics, vaccines, devices, diagnostics, and other biomedical products on the market originating from this research. This societal benefit is believed to be the truest measure of the value and importance of licensing and technology transfer from research institutions.

Case Study: Licensing of HPV vaccine technology by NIH and Georgetown University

Human papillomavirus (HPV) vaccine is a vaccine that prevents infection with certain species of human papillomavirus associated with the development of cervical cancer, genital warts, and some less common cancers. Although most women infected with genital HPV will not have complications from the virus, worldwide there are an estimated 470,000 new cases of cervical cancer that result in 233,000 deaths per year. About eighty percent of deaths from cervical cancer occur in poor countries.

The research that led to the development of the vaccine began in the 1980s by groups primarily at the University of Rochester, Georgetown University, the German Cancer Center (DKFZ) and the NIH. Medimmune, Inc., then a very small development stage vaccine company based in Gaithersburg, Maryland, licensed the HPV vaccine technology available from all four institutions in the early 1990s. This work, and the work of others, eventually became the basis of Gardasil® (sold by Merck) and Cervarix® (sold by GSK)—blockbuster products in terms of public health and market impacts.

REFERENCES

1. See "NIH Overview" at www.nih.gov/about/NIHoverview.html
2. See Association of University Technology Managers (AUTM), "AUTM Annual Licensing Survey" at www.autm.net
3. Gil Ben-Menachem, Steven M. Ferguson and Krishna Balakrishnan, "Doing Business With NIH", Nature Biotechnology , volume 24, number 1, pp.17-20 (January 2006)
4. Steven M. Ferguson, "Products, Partners and Public Health: Transfer of Biomedical Technologies from the U.S. Government", Journal of Biolaw & Business, volume 5, number 2 pp.35-39 (2002)
5. Robert S. MacWright, "The University of Virginia Patent Foundation: A Midsized Technology Transfer Foundation Focused on Faculty Service, Operated Using a Deal-Based Business Model", AUTM Technology Transfer Practice Manual, 3rd Edition, Volume 2, Chapter 2.3a, pp. 1-21
6. Ibid., see also www.spinnertech.com.
7. See the "University Start-ups" annual conferences held by the National Center for Entrepreneurial Technology Transfer (NCET2) at www.ncet2.org
8. See also conferences and webinars on this topic organized by the National Center for Entrepreneurial Technology Transfer (NCET2) at www.ncet2.org
9. In addition top grant awards, business and technical assistance is available to firms participating in these programs which can be combined with technologies licensed from a federal or university lab. A most promising development is the new "bridge awards" being made by some agencies to increase the likelihood of eventual venture funding. See www.sbir.gov for details.
10. Jonathan J. Jensen, Katrine Wyller , Eric R. London, Sabarni K. Chatterjee, Fiona E. Murray, Mark L. Rohrbaugh and Ashley J. Stevens, "The Contribution of Public Sector Research to the Discovery of New Drugs", Poster at AUTM Annual Conference (2007)
11. David Roessner, Jennifer Bond, Sumiye Okubo and Mark Planting, "The Economic Impact of Licensed Commercialized Inventions Originating in University Research, 1996-2007", Final Report to the Biotechnology Industry Organization (September 3, 2009), available at www.bio.org

CHAPTER 8

Regulatory Affairs

Libbie Mansell, PhD, MBA, RAC
President, White Oak BioPharma Solutions, LLC

INTRODUCTION

Product development is a lengthy, risky, and expensive endeavor. Many innovative technologies exist that are ready for, and amenable to, development—be they your brainchild, or in-licensed from others. Still, entrepreneurs need to attract substantial resources—funding and product development talent—to ensure corporate success. Likewise, buy-side stakeholders considering potential investment in a new technology must carefully consider the viability and economic return associated with a product candidate. Since the regulatory environment is complex and dynamic, entrepreneurs and investors alike should understand the many important aspects of regulatory affairs that can affect their asset(s) technically and financially. Successful navigation of the domestic and international regulatory landscape during the full spectrum of product development will ensure good management of scarce and valuable resources. Further, it will ensure that regulatory milestones are aligned with business milestones and, consequently, value inflection points—the accomplishments that significantly and rapidly enhance the perceived value of a company. An entrepreneur with a clear, accurate, and sophisticated regulatory strategy differentiates themselves in a very positive manner.

This chapter is intended to provide readers with practical information regarding the regulated environment in which they will work. Although some newly formed companies may independently conduct late-stage development and seek marketing approval for their product candidates, most focus their efforts from discovery through Phase IIa. A Phase IIa human study is a[n] pilot/initial clinical trial to evaluate both benefit [efficacy] and safety in a selected patient population. Partnering with, or out-licensing to, larger companies for later stage activities often provides needed expertise, and creates another exit strategy option with an attractive return on investment. Hence, this chapter will focus on regulatory aspects most pertinent to early- and mid-stage development for product candidates in the life sciences: biologics, small molecules, medical devices, diagnostics, and combinations thereof. Key regulatory elements affecting a company's development progress, funding, and corporate success will be covered. This discussion is intended to provide issue awareness, and care has been taken to minimize legal and regulatory jargon for clarity. More comprehensive treatises of covered topics can be found if additional details are desired, and excellent introductions to the manufacturing, marketing, and post-approval regulatory environment exist elsewhere.

As entrepreneurs consider a technology for development, they must understand what products are regulated, how, and by which entities. Marketing opportunities exist internationally for innovative products—so knowledge of the *global* regulatory landscape is important. Although regulatory concepts are usually similar, laws, regulations, and guidance can differ substantially between countries and the entrepreneur must identify those that apply to demonstrate good stewardship of the technology and company resources. Additionally, special country-specific development and regulatory paradigms provide useful benefits—if utilized correctly. Knowing when and how to effectively communicate with health authorities is imperative for the start-up company.

Entrepreneurs will learn the value and benefits of creating a comprehensive regulatory strategy. This chapter, and the analytical work required to produce it, provides a viable and efficient pathway to registration that guides daily project activities in a company. The pathway also demonstrates that the product candidate is approvable and could supply an acceptable, even attractive, return on investment to stakeholders. Identifying and partnering with qualified regulatory affairs professionals is a critical success element for founders and entrepreneurs. Regulatory personnel must be skilled in numerous regulatory sub-disciplines, international procedures, negotiations, and all facets of product research and development. The right individual or group brings expertise that can streamline development and subsequent regulatory review activities.

WHICH PRODUCTS ARE REGULATED

As an entrepreneur starts considering product development, it is helpful to understand which products are regulated and to what extent. The product descriptions that follow are intended to define general characteristics and introduce key regulatory framework differences. The spectrum runs from notifying a regulatory agency of safety information to full application, review, and approval procedures. International variations are extensive, and the reader is strongly encouraged to seek country-specific details early in product development.

DRUGS (PHARMACEUTICALS) AND BIOLOGICS

A drug/biologic is any substance or mixture of substances used for the diagnosis, treatment, mitigation or prevention of a disease, disorder, abnormal physical state, or its symptoms in humans or animals. Many regulatory agencies regard radiopharmaceuticals and biologics as drugs; some agencies have separate reviewing divisions for these products. Radiopharmaceuticals are drugs with unstable nuclei that spontaneously disintegrate, emitting nuclear particles or energy. Biologics are drugs prepared using a biological starting or source material derived from micro-organism, viral, animal, or human materials and produced using conventional or recombinant DNA methods.

A product license or approved marketing application is generally required to introduce small molecules and biologics into public commerce. The usual standard for licensure or approval involves adequately demonstrating safety, efficacy, purity, and control of manufacturing.

MEDICAL DEVICES AND *IN VITRO* DIAGNOSTICS

A medical device is any article, instrument, or apparatus (or any component, part, or accessory thereof) used in the diagnosis, treatment, mitigation or prevention of a disease, disorder, abnormal physical state, or its symptoms in humans or animals. Devices restore, correct, or modify a body function or structure.

Many health authorities regulate these products on a risk-based classification system that categorizes product candidates on invasiveness and the level of regulatory control necessary to assure their safety and effectiveness (*e.g.*, Class I, II, III, IV in Canada and Japan). *In vitro* diagnostics may be reviewed by a separate office or division, but usually under the same classification scheme as devices. Devices in the lowest risk category, such as surgical instruments, usually only require agency notification of certain information for marketing, but may have other regulatory obligations. Higher class designations have more rigorous development and approval criteria. Entrepreneurs will immediately recognize the importance of correct classification since it dictates the application process and level of development effort required. Early advice from regulatory experts on classification should guide development and application activities.

Regulation of combination products, such as drug-device or biologic-device, is more complicated than either individual product type, since technical review issues arise from multiple sources. Jurisdiction issues for review and evaluation responsibilities are usually resolved based on the product's mechanism of action. Combinations are often very attractive to entrepreneurs, investors, and other stakeholders, since they utilize the most beneficial features of different technologies, such as the efficacy of a drug plus the targeted delivery of a device.

MEDICAL DEVICE DATA SYSTEMS

Regulation of computer and software products intended to transmit data from devices is a relatively new category for regulatory agencies around the world. For example, medical device data systems have not been actively regulated in the U.S., but the FDA proposes to do so by assigning these products a Class I designation and requiring the lowest level of oversight.[1] This action is under heavy debate given the numerous jurisdictional, technical, and implementation issues.

BOTANICALS

These products contain vegetable matter, and constitute a very active development area—especially internationally—where botanicals have enjoyed a long history of use in traditional medicine. In some countries, little or no regulations apply because appropriate use of these products has been established for decades, even centuries. Western countries tend to classify botanicals either as: (a) drugs subject to premarket review and assessment via a license application, or (b) as homeopathic/natural products requiring only agency notification (*e.g.*, Canada, U.S.). This distinction is based on whether medical claims are sought and/or additional non-homeopathic ingredients are incorporated into the final product.[2] Establishment requirements exist in some countries regardless of the market access procedure. Entrepreneurs should be aware that many health authorities house review expertise for botanical products separately from drug divisions.

DIETARY OR FOOD SUPPLEMENTS

Supplements include vitamins, minerals, herbs, botanicals, amino acids, and metabolites intended to augment the diet—but are not intended to treat, diagnose, cure, or mitigate the effects of disease. Prevention, treatment, or curative marketing claims generally elevate the product to drug status. A notification process (for safety information) and/or an establishment license will usually suffice for marketing dietary supplements, unless the product is chemically altered. It is unclear if extraction and concentration constitute chemical alteration in most countries.[3] Many unclear areas exist in the regulations given the introduction of nutraceuticals. In the U.S., good manufacturing procedures have recently been established for dietary supplements, the implementation of which can significantly affect the regulatory strategy for some entrepreneurs.

HUMAN CELLS, TISSUES, AND RELATED PRODUCTS (HCT/Ps)

Tissue-engineered products restore, maintain, or improve the function of human tissues and organs. These often include, for example, bone, heart valves, urinary or liver prostheses, and stem cells. Disease transmission following transplant raises the safety risk for these products. Consequently, many countries use a tiered, risk-based, regulatory framework for these products. Minimally-manipulated products manufactured for autologous use (*e.g.*, vascular grafts) are subject to very little regulation in the U.S., while highly modified products intended for allogenic use (*e.g.*, bone material) require a marketing application prior to commercialization (4). The latter are regulated as drugs, biologics, or medical devices because they carry higher safety risk of disease transmission.

Entrepreneurs familiar with drug and device production issues—and having such understanding only works to your benefit—recognize that current good manufacturing procedures and quality system regulations do not adequately control HCT/Ps. Consequently, regulations for donor eligibility, methods of recovery, implementation of meaningful quality programs, equipment and facilities, environmental control and monitoring, tissue receipt and storage, as well as shipping and distribution continue to be modified. The European Union (EU) and U.S. are actively adjusting their regulatory framework to accommodate HCT/Ps.

Stem cell development currently constitutes the most difficult and confusing product area for regulators. Entrepreneurs innovating in this area should be apprised of the regulatory spectrum that exists. Some countries (*e.g.*, Greece) have no legislation on regulating these products, while others (*e.g.*, Germany) prohibit research for these products altogether.

NANOTECHNOLOGY

Nanotechnology is another new field for regulators, meaning that there is little precedence to guide entrepreneurs in the path to commercialization. Many countries lack the regulatory framework to specifically address these products—but are evaluating them on a case-by-base basis.[5] Nanomaterials are known to have different and unusual physical and chemical properties compared to their macromaterial counterparts. These differences may be advantageously applied to medical product development.

However, there are still gaps in technical understanding, and the potential safety risks associated with nanomaterials are not well-characterized.[6] Current regulations and guidances are under evaluation and revision to improve their applicability to products using nanotechnology. Entrepreneurs and scientists in this field are concerned that new regulation, when available, may not be pragmatic and therefore stifle medical product innovation—an anathema to the public health mission of every country.

COSMETICS

A cosmetic is any substance or mixture of substances used in cleansing, improving, or altering the complexion, skin, nails, hair or teeth. It includes products such as deodorants and perfumes. Commercialization occurs through a notification system in most countries—although many regulatory unclear areas exist given the popularity of "cosmeceuticals" and the medical claims associated with these products.

REGULATORY AGENCIES AND HOW THEY WORK

Regulatory agencies around the world have a similar mission: to protect and enhance the health of its citizens—in part by regulating medical products available to the public. Health authorities around the world are organized differently. In some regions, health authorities have expansive sanitation and social support resources but limited medical product evaluation capabilities. Other countries have extremely sophisticated and scientifically-driven review, evaluation, and public policy functions. The spectrum can be frustrating to entrepreneurs. Regardless of the health authorities' priorities, each is governed by its own set of laws and regulations.

Laws are usually drafted and enacted by a country's legislative body in the form of Acts or Directives. They set policy in general terms, and non-compliance results in criminal penalties.[7] Most governments provide for a regulatory agency to interpret and implement their laws consistently. Consequently, regulations are developed to instruct its citizens on how to comply with established laws. Non-compliance with regulations typically results in costly and time-consuming remediation. Laws and regulations enacted in each country establish the standard by which product candidates will be evaluated and approved for marketing. For example, in the U.S., sponsors must demonstrate a product is safe, effective, pure or free from defects, and manufactured under strict controls. It is a common misconception that this legal regulatory standard is favorably altered for government-based product sponsors (*e.g.*, the National Institutes of Health) or public-private partnerships.

Guidelines (*e.g.*, guidance for industry, points to consider) do not carry the full force or penalty of laws and regulations. Guidelines are intended to provide the best current thinking of a regulatory body at the time these documents are issued. They are published on a myriad of specific regulatory and development topics of interest to sponsors. Although considered voluntary, there is an expectation of adherence to guidelines. Hence, entrepreneurs should carefully assess which available documents are appropriate for their product candidates. Alternatively, companies must provide clear, well-substantiated justifications in correspondence with health authorities when seemingly applicable guidelines are deemed inappropriate by the company.

Different agency structures, processes, and regulations also affect the frequency and type of communications between company and health authorities. Agencies usually specify details for site meetings, telephone and fax communications, and written correspondence. Some regulatory authorities are interactive and transparent; others less so. Entrepreneurs should create a communication plan that matches the company's information needs and reporting obligations with agency processes and expectations. Face-to-face meetings are an opportunity to establish consensus on key development or application issues—so companies should prepare emergent, substantive questions for joint discussions. An additional benefit to face-to-face meetings is the chance to develop a deeper relationship between parties than can be accomplished remotely. This relationship can facilitate communication—although, of course, it will not impact the company's need to comply with all relevant regulations.

Some country specifics follow:

UNITED STATES

The U.S. Food and Drug Administration (FDA) is organized by product type (Centers), and then by therapeutic area (offices, divisions). Efforts continue to harmonize review and evaluation processes across offices and divisions where possible, but each is allowed substantial latitude and flexibility to operate in a manner consistent with their mission to protect and enhance public health.

Applications required to initiate a company's initial U.S. clinical trial (first-in-human study) are reviewed via a negative vetting process, and may occur simultaneously with internal review board applications. Once in effect, the investigational new drug application (IND) or investigational device exemption (IDE) provides the mechanism through which FDA communications take place. The IND and IDE also provide a legal exemption from the usual need to have FDA approval before patients can receive a medical product. The FDA is considered relatively transparent. Typically, it encourages communications with the entity responsible for the study (sponsor) when development issues arise; entrepreneurs should avail themselves of this privilege when appropriate. However, the reader must appreciate the FDA is not a company's consultant; companies should provide scientifically and medically justifiable solutions to facilitate productive discussions with FDA officials. As development proceeds, the IND/IDE is amended with study protocols, final reports, safety data, and chemistry, manufacturing and controls (CMC) changes, etc., until all approval requirements are met and a marketing application is filed.

Marketing applications include new drug applications (NDA), biologics license applications (BLA), premarket notification or premarket approval applications (PMA) for devices, and abbreviated new drug applications (ANDA) for generic drugs. Use of the electronic common technical document (eCTD) format is encouraged for biologics and drugs, and an electronic format is under consideration for devices. The entrepreneur's key to a one-cycle review is minimizing the potential for review queries and delays by providing robust data sets and comprehensive documentation to demonstrate safety, effectiveness, purity, and control of manufacture. Hence, correctly identifying and executing early/mid-stage development activities are crucial.

The FDA frequently uses its advisory committee system to obtain guidance on application issues. Entrepreneurs should understand that while advisory committees do not have approval authority, their recommendations are usually adopted by FDA personnel authorized to make approval decisions. Anticipating the concerns of an advisory committee helps a start-up company "front-load" a development program with early studies to address and even mitigate questions from regulators and their affiliated advisors. Most advisory committee meeting minutes are available to the public, providing valuable competitive and regulatory intelligence.

EUROPE

Countries in the EU have their own national health authorities, such as the United Kingdom's Medicines and Healthcare Products Regulatory Agency and Germany's Bundesinstitut für Arzneimittel und Medizenprodukte. Each authority is responsible for interpreting and implementing European Commission Directives into individual national laws and regulations. The European Medicines Agency (EMA) is not a health authority *per se,* but rather serves as an oversight and coordinating body for community-wide product candidate applications and reviews. This agency also creates guidelines for industry on product development topics.

Companies can request scientific advice from individual health authorities or the EMA if difficult development issues arise requiring health authority discussions. Although substantial fees are associated with EMA advice, this may be the only mechanism for resolving questions if publicly available information (*e.g.,* guidance documents, experts and consultants, European Public Assessment Reports) is not sufficient. Small and medium-sized companies may be eligible for substantial fee reductions, but entrepreneurs should balance the need for formal scientific advice with costs required to obtain it. Entrepreneurs should note EMA advice is non-binding, yet represents the best counsel available at the time it is given.

Companies wishing to conduct human studies in Europe must submit a clinical trial application (CTA) to the health authority in the country where the study will be conducted. The first CTA must also include an investigational medical products application. The company receives either a positive or negative response after CTA review by a national authority. Products are considered for approval when a marketing authorization application—there are several types—is submitted and evaluated by a health authority via the centralized, decentralized, mutual recognition, or national authorization procedures. Critical attention should be paid to which procedure is used, since they each have unique features, limitations, advantages, timetables, and eligibility criteria. Devices gaining market access using community-wide regulations and approval are given the European Conformity (CE) mark. Entrepreneurs are prudent to seek advice from regulatory experts for the details and subtleties associated with all procedures and applications so these can be incorporated into early development plans.

JAPAN

Japan's Ministry of Health, Labour, and Welfare (MHLW) has assigned responsibility for scientific reviews of medical products, clinical trial system oversight, conformity audits, and industry consultations to the Pharmaceutical and Medical Devices Agency (PMDA, Sogo-kiko). The decision on marketing authorization remains with the MHLW, however, following receipt of a review report from the PMDA. The PMDA is divided into offices based on product type to ensure specific expertise is applied to product data review and consultations.

The PMDA administers a clinical trial notification system. This agency is noted for their data package assessments following completion of non-clinical, Phase I, and Phase II programs, as well as pre-NDA consultation. Further enhancements to its scientific consultation process include coverage of all development matters—not just clinical trial planning and NDA-directed discussions. Companies should be aware of Japan-specific approval requirements as they plan development programs for innovative products. For example, the PMDA requires conduct of a Phase I study and, possibly, a registration trial in Japan. Bridging study requirements have frequently frustrated entrepreneurs' development plans. Multinational trials also remain a challenge, given Japan's strong reliance on physician researchers having limited experience with documentation requirements from other countries. Marketing applications are made in eCTD format. Devices applications follow notification, certification, or approval procedures depending on the product classification.

The Japanese government has recently revised its pharmaceutical affairs law (PAL). An excellent summary of the PAL is available from the Japanese Pharmaceutical Manufacturers Association[8], and is highly recommended to entrepreneurs wishing to conduct drug development or obtain marketing approval in Japan.

CANADA

Health Canada has assigned responsibility for scientific reviews of medical products, clinical trial system oversight, and industry consultations to the health products and food branch (HPFB). Like other major agencies, the HPFB is divided into directorates based generally on product type and regulatory activity (*e.g.*, inspections, policy development). Specialized activities are further coordinated in bureaus and offices.

Directorate, bureau, and office personnel frequently meet with companies on product development program issues, and entrepreneurs are encouraged to seek their counsel to obviate missing Canada-specific regulatory elements. Clinical trial initiation in Canada requires submission of a formal application to the appropriate product directorate. Companies are officially notified, after review, if applications are approved or rejected. New drug submissions (NDSs), required for marketing authorization, use the CTD format. This enables a company to start building their marketing application early in development as studies and experiments are completed. Device license applications initiate the marketing authorization process for device and *in vitro* diagnostic products.

CHINA, INDIA, RUSSIA, BRAZIL, AND OTHERS

Many regulatory agencies around the world are rapidly enhancing their review and evaluation, monitoring, and administrative capabilities. Improvements have been made following proactive efforts to learn from more established health authorities via personnel secondments, meetings, symposia, and joint working groups.[9] Some countries are more active than others in international regulatory collaborations and prominent trade organizations.

Companies should not assume, however, that product development programs created to align with regulations from more prominent health authorities will be acceptable elsewhere. Substantial time delays for application reviews exist in many countries due to highly variable regulations. Also, a few countries have not fully clarified responsibilities and administrative operations within their regulatory agencies. For example, China has strong provincial governments and product developers remain confused on which oversight responsibilities are assigned to them versus which remain under central government control.[10] Entrepreneurs should identify any costly sequential or duplicative development requirements early in development to ensure appropriate data is collected for a marketing application and delays to project timelines are minimized.

Since mechanisms for formal agency interactions are often unclear, companies may have difficulty determining required data elements. For example, importing clinical trial materials into Brazil requires an important license specific to a given batch and shipment. Regulatory predictability and efficiency remains uncertain for these countries, but continued improvements are expected.

SMALL AND EMERGING MARKETS

Venture philanthropy (most basically, the funding of for-profit entities by charitable foundations) are a relatively new funding source for entrepreneurs. Support is usually given for disease-specific commercial development to expedite the movement of products from bench to bedside. Many of these organizations facilitate product development for diseases representing major, unmet medical needs with blockbuster (revenue) potential. In addition, other foundations support such development for medical needs prevalent in resource-constrained countries where national competent health authorities have little or no capacity to regulate medicinal products. Countries with nascent regulatory authorities often adopt the World Health Organization's (WHO) certification scheme, or parts thereof, to facilitate registration and approval of important medical products.

Major health authorities participating in the WHO program provide certificates of pharmaceutical product (U.S.) or certificates of medicinal product (EU) following product approval in the certifying country, and upon company request. The issued certificate signifies a complete assessment of the quality, safety and effectiveness of a medical product—and each certifying authority agrees to inform the WHO and the nascent regulatory body of safety or quality issues that arise with the product.[11] Alternatively, export certificates may be issued for products intended to treat diseases which do not occur in the certifying country. Hence, a variety of processes are available to entrepreneurs wishing to develop and market new products in regions with smaller regulatory authorities.

The certification scheme can be complex to navigate. National applications often require additional information from certifying countries (*e.g.*, labeling, published assessment reports)—but each certifying country has committed to providing only certain official documents as part of the certification process. There are situations when nascent health authorities need certification only for certain development disciples (*e.g.*, CMC) or multiple certificates. Hence, a sophisticated understanding of international approval requirements and access to major health authority information is required for successful use of WHO's certification scheme. Entrepreneurs should understand the context of the certificate in other countries' registration paradigms so they can design development programs accordingly.

Small and emerging markets have a higher incidence of unusual requirements. In many countries, a clear policy of established requirements does not exist; development and approval occur on a case-by-base basis. Entrepreneurs should plan for differences in ethics standards, data security and health record privacy, importation, and local manufacturing requirements. When thinking of a business strategy, these regulatory challenges should give an entrepreneur pause. For potential investors and corporate alliance partners, the smaller market in the developing world can be—by itself—problematic. Factor in the added regulatory risk inherent in the developing world, and there has to be compelling reasons to justify pursuit of such a difficult path.

Most resource-constrained countries recognize the importance of protecting intellectual property, but reserve the right to implement compulsory licensing under the international Agreement on Trade Related Aspects of Intellectual Property Rights (TRIPS) for products deemed necessary to avert or minimize a public health emergency. TRIPS allows each country defines what constitutes a public health emergency. So, international trade agreements will not necessarily protect an entrepreneur's intellectual property status.

ICH AND GHTF

The International Conference on Harmonization of Technical Requirements for Registration of Pharmaceuticals for Human Use (ICH) and the Global Harmonization Task Force (GHTF) are international standard-setting organizations for drug and device industries, respectively. Although they are not regulatory authorities *per se*, their mission is highly regarded by regulatory agencies around the world. Thus, entrepreneurs considering entering markets outside the U.S. should be familiar with them.

These organizations are comprised of industry and regulatory agency personnel from the most established markets and include additional participants as frequent advisors. For example, Canada is an observer to ICH, providing frequent advice to permanent EU, U.S., and Japanese members. Scientific, medical, and technical matters affecting product registration are discussed in working parties, and mutually acceptable procedures and standards are identified to streamline registration while assuring product quality/conformance, safety, and effectiveness. Although ICH and GHTF compliance is voluntary, and interpretation of their guidances varies between regulators, entrepreneurs should understand that such compliance is highly encouraged.

AN ADDITIONAL NOTE

Authorities in many countries do not officially mandate product prices after approval. Nonetheless, their government reimbursement plans have established criteria for product qualification. Reimbursement decisions can substantially affect product penetration and, therefore, potential revenues. Although a discussion of international pricing mechanisms is beyond the scope of this chapter, entrepreneurs are advised to carefully consider collecting data during development that justifies advantageous pricing for their product following approval. Most major metropolitan areas have professional advisors with core skills in reimbursement. Such professionals are often associated with management consulting or legal firms.

SPECIAL DEVELOPMENT PROCEDURES & REVIEW PARADIGMS

It is important for entrepreneurs to understand how special regulatory paradigms and review mechanisms may benefit their product candidates. Appropriate use of these special programs can, in many cases, accelerate development or regulatory review, and provide companies with economic and business advantages. Entrepreneurs may use the applicability of a special paradigm to choose among available technologies during the start-up phase. Strategic partners—funders and developers—also look for products eligible for these programs. Therefore, such savvy, out-of-the-box thinking may enhance a company's ability to acquire funding, minimize development risk, and attract future development partners.

Like companies in the medical product industries, health authorities also want to improve public access to new, life-saving therapies. This is especially true for products that represent the first available treatment or products with advantages over existing therapies. For example, in the U.S., the FDA has developed priority review, accelerated approval, and fast track approaches to make innovative and/or improved drugs for serious, life-threatening conditions available to patients as quickly as possible. Many countries have similar programs. It must be noted, however, that these paradigms do not change the approval standard of demonstrating safety and effectiveness.

ACCELERATED APPROVAL

Based on ICH guidance[12], most countries will consider commonly accepted surrogate endpoints as the basis of establishing efficacy for certain product approvals. A surrogate endpoint is a biomarker or laboratory parameter, found coincident with a medical condition that improves or worsens depending on the course of the disease. For example, viral load and tumor shrinkage have been surrogates for mortality for some HIV and cancer therapies, respectively. Eligibility for accelerated approval is based on two criteria: (a) the product candidate must treat a serious, life-threatening or debilitating illness for which no (or much less effective) therapeutic options exist, and (b) epidemiologic, therapeutic, pathophysiologic, or other scientific support suggests the surrogate is reasonably likely to predict clinical benefit.

A surrogate endpoint is used in lieu of a clinically meaningful measure of patient benefit (*e.g.*, survival, symptom improvement) that directly measures how a patient feels or functions, but may take substantial time to manifest during a clinical trial. In practice, surrogate endpoints decrease the duration of efficacy studies and, therefore, the overall development time. However, these endpoints are considered controversial since they can mislead regulators and healthcare practitioners about the nature and magnitude of the true efficacy effect.[13] Biomarkers may be useful in early development. They can provide clues to particular sub-populations of patients (more) likely to achieve treatment benefit—thus helping guide product development strategy. However, they are usually unacceptable for registration-directed clinical trials—later-stage trials are often seen as the last step prior to seeking marketing approval. Validating surrogate endpoints is time-consuming, and product approvals based on them are "conditional" in many countries, with substantial post-approval obligations including one or more confirmatory trials. Given these liabilities, the possible use of a surrogate measure should be discussed with regulatory authorities early in development.

FAST TRACK

A fast track designation is granted by regulatory authorities for serious or life-threatening illness with unmet medical need. A company must apply for and receive the designation to be eligible for its benefits. Benefits vary from country to country, but usually include more agency consultations, some form of priority (i.e., expedited) review status, and accelerated approval. In the U.S., a fast track designation allows a company to file a "rolling" marketing application (i.e., application components are submitted sequentially, rather than simultaneously). Health Canada is considering a progressive licensing scheme to fast track new products through abbreviated late-stage development in exchange for increased post-market surveillance.

PRIORITY REVIEW

A priority review designation is given to drugs and devices that offer major advances in treatment, diagnosis, or prevention—or that provide alternative treatment where no adequate therapy currently exists. Products that eliminate or reduce a treatment-limiting adverse effect associated with currently available treatments may also qualify. However, eligibility may be restricted in some countries to products for serious and debilitating diseases.

Generally, a priority review must be requested by the company at the time the marketing application is submitted. It usually follows discussions with regulators at a pre-application meeting. The key feature and benefit of a priority review is the shortened duration of regulatory review for a marketing application (*e.g.*, 180 days in the U.S. and Canada). Still, entrepreneurs and founders should be aware that substantial queries and difficulties with a priority review application may preclude a shortened review.

ORPHAN DESIGNATION

Orphan drug programs are intended to encourage development of therapeutic products for rare and neglected diseases that are serious and life-threatening. These product/indication combinations have historically been unattractive to entrepreneurs because future revenues for such treatments rarely justify development costs. Recently, however, some products for smaller markets have been able to charge enough per patient to provide an acceptable return to investors. Consequently, those looking at exploit smaller markets should examine comparables and those companies' record of financial success or difficulty.

Most major regulatory agencies have specific programs for orphan products. Some agencies have combined efforts to facilitate orphan product development internationally through common application systems. Interestingly, Canada does not have an established orphan drug program, but instead fosters development for these products through Health Canada's priority review and surrogate endpoint programs.

Eligibility criteria and development requirements vary internationally. For example, rare diseases are defined as those affecting fewer than 200,000 in the U.S., 2,000 in Australia, 50,000 in Japan, or 0.05% of patients in the EU. A product may be eligible for orphan designation if it represents the first therapeutic available to treat a rare disease or demonstrates clinical superiority over existing therapies. These may be new products or new indications for previously approved products. Benefits associated with an orphan designation generally include government grants for development work, corporate tax credits (some with carry-back, carry-forward provisions), exemption from application fees, and marketing exclusivity. Hence, entrepreneurs and their investors should assess the value of country-specific economic and development advantages associated with these products.

505(b)(2)

The U.S. has legal provisions in the regulatory framework for a "hybrid" marketing application when certain modifications are made to previously approved drugs. This application type is more commonly known as a 505(b)(2), in reference to the location in the Food, Drug, and Cosmetic Act where it is described. Few entrepreneurs are familiar with the 505(b)(2) application despite its increased use in recent years and the numerous benefits it can provide to a company. More than 50% of drugs approved in 2008 used a 505(b)(2) application process.[14] Consequently, when applicable, this type of application represents a highly beneficial commercialization path for entrepreneurs to explore.

Hybrid applications share features of both new drug and abbreviated new drug applications for generic products. As with all new drug applications, the 505(b)(2) application must include substantial evidence of safety and efficacy—the regulatory standard for all product approvals. As with generic drug applications, a company may rely on the FDA's previous findings of safety and effectiveness for the previously approved drug, to the extent these findings apply to the modified product. In practice, this means the major body of development work conducted for the previously approved product need not be duplicated for the modified product. Only new efficacy and safety data applicable to the modification are needed to supplement previous findings referenced in the 505(b)(2) application. The reader will immediately appreciate this approach can substantially streamline development activities, decrease development costs and risks, and shorten the time to market.

It is important for entrepreneurs to understand that the 505(b)(2) application must include an additional clinical trial other than a bioequivalence/bioavailability (BE/BA) study. It may be tempting to conduct only a BE/BA study as a bridge to the original product's findings of safety and effectiveness. However, such a strategy disqualifies a modified product from the 505(b)(2) process and the three-year marketing exclusivity benefit associated with it. Hence, careful regulatory analysis must be completed early in product development on the modifications allowed and studies required for this paradigm.

THE REGULATORY STRATEGY

The regulatory strategy describes the development process or pathway necessary to achieve efficient and advantageous product registration. It provides logistical details on major studies and experiments, regulatory milestones, and specific outcomes needed to demonstrate the product's safety, effectiveness, purity or lack of defects, and manufacturing controls. The regulatory strategy also includes strategic analysis of key issues with the potential to affect development and registration (*e.g.*, public policy and legislative activities).

Major issues and challenges are also included to ensure appropriate actions are taken to minimize negative effects to the product candidate's future value. The regulatory strategy is a major component of the overall product development plan, and requires inputs from and outputs to individual pre-clinical, clinical, non-clinical, manufacturing, and marketing/business sectors within a company.

VALUE TO ENTREPRENEUR AND PARTNERS

Financial resources are usually limited in a start-up company. Even a more mature company with some investments or resources still needs to closely monitor and control cash flow. Therefore, strategic or logistical mistakes during development can have dire consequences for a young venture. The regulatory strategy protects the product program after the entrepreneur is able to overcome early funding challenges and, in many cases, survived the "valley of death"—the transition from a government- or self-funding phase to, most often, equity investment. The regulatory strategy is the roadmap for generating all data required to meet regulatory standards for product approval, including safety, effectiveness, purity/lack of defects, and control of manufacture. It details the manner in which studies should be conducted to support the most commercially attractive indication and professional labeling possible. Costly mistakes in these areas are avoided by aligning and tracking company operations against the pathway to registration described in this document. Hence, a comprehensive and accurate regulatory strategy is a seminal corporate document for entrepreneurs—as well as those who have been through the process many times.

A solid regulatory strategy also demonstrates the credibility of the entrepreneur, leadership team, and company to investors or future development partners. It aligns regulatory milestones with value-inflection points—the accomplishments, such as initiation of a first-in-human study—that quickly and substantially increase a company's perceived value. A viable and efficient path to registration must be available and articulated for the product candidate to have value for other partners. Hence, the regulatory strategy can attract later-stage development partners and investors. Future development partners seek in-licensing candidates with a high probability of approval and potential for adding revenues to their financial statements. Investors want to ensure their product candidates will provide an acceptable exit strategy and return on investment; this may be in the form of an initial public offering for the company, purchase by a larger development partner, or marketing approval resulting in sales revenue. A well-constructed regulatory strategy demonstrates the company's preparedness and conveys the likelihood of a company's good stewardship of a partner's resources.

CONTENTS

The contents of a regulatory strategy depend on product type and therapeutic area. Most provide plans for the entire course of development, although some entrepreneurs prefer to limit the scope to include activities for the next few major milestones. Abbreviated regulatory strategies focus on near-term events to the exclusion of later-stage, outsourced activities; these are less helpful for investor and alliance discussions. Entrepreneurs should be aware the best outcomes are planned in reverse chronology and based on previous regulatory experience.

Some important components requiring a comprehensive analysis in the regulatory strategy include:

- Regulatory milestones and timelines for all countries of interest, including global submissions
- Communication/interaction plan for regulatory agencies and their affiliates
- Identification of all product approval requirements
- Analysis of pertinent guidances and special regulatory programs
- Competitive intelligence from review and analysis of precedent products, official approval summary documents from regulatory agencies on similar products, advisory committee meeting minutes, known competitors' development programs
- Desired labeling claims and optimized labeling language (target product profile)

- Applicable marketing and data exclusivities
- Impact of state and federal legislative issues; public policy issues
- Clinical studies required to meet registration standards, including endpoints, trial design features, and statistical plan for data analysis
- Implications of product's safety profile on registration; pharmacovigilance and surveillance planning
- Pediatric and special patient sub-population plans
- Preclinical package requirements to demonstrate safe introduction into human trials and sufficient long-term safety profile
- Manufacturing plans that coordinate with non-clinical/clinical needs and marketing objectives
- Quality and compliance aspects
- Special needs for reimbursement and pricing
- Program risk evaluation and mitigation planning

Each of these topics needs to account for the specific requirements in each country for which commercialization is desired. In practice, the regulatory strategy is a complex document that coordinates numerous, often divergent, regulatory landscapes in which the entrepreneur will work.

REVISIONS

Data acquired as experiments and studies are completed inform the next steps in the development pathway. The regulatory strategy should be updated to account for any changes to future development program that may be warranted based on new data. Consequently, regulatory strategies are dynamic documents that undergo frequent review for continued applicability; appropriate revision demonstrates prudent guardianship of the product candidate. Entrepreneurs, and any product developer, needs to be comfortable with the ever-evolving nature of regulatory documents and submissions.

AUTHORSHIP

The regulatory affairs professional authors the strategy with input from a those in research and development, operations, manufacturing, legal, and business. (Marketing may be a component for those products with shorter commercialization paths. Typically, companies more than a few years from regulatory approval are too early to commit such resources.) Founders or entrepreneurs sometimes write this document if they have extensive regulatory experience. Implementation of the regulatory strategy follows authorization from management personnel who are chiefly responsible for development and business activities.

HIRING REGULATORY PERSONNEL

The value of regulatory expertise is frequently underestimated by entrepreneurs and founders. Knowledge of the value-add tends to lag behind other key components such as legal and business/financial help. However, the assistance of an experienced professional often makes the difference between providing a credible corporate image to the investment community, regulatory agencies, etc., and failing to provide the necessary gravitas to successfully engage these groups. For example, company references to an "approved" U.S. IND expose an entrepreneur's regulatory naïveté since the FDA's review process precedes approval and INDs "go into effect". This simple error compromises the entrepreneur's credibility when externally presenting other regulatory or development plans. A glaring lack of sophistication is sufficient for an investor or pharmaceutical business development profession to move on to the next business plan or technical summary.

PERMANENT EMPLOYEE OR CONSULTANT

Hiring a regulatory affairs professional will be one of the entrepreneur's most important personnel decisions. Both hiring paradigms—permanent employee or contracted consultant—have advantages and limitations that must be carefully considered. Obviously, permanent employees receive a recurrent salary, benefits, office space and equipment, etc., and they are dedicated entirely to the company's development activities. Alternatively, consultants work on an hourly or retained fee structure under an established contract, and have a demonstrated ability to function effectively in the virtual environment typical of many new start-up companies. They work either independently or as a member of a collaborative network or small corporation with a full-spectrum of regulatory disciplines. Both permanent employees and consultants may contribute in other development disciplines, depending on their training. The need for product- or therapeutic area-specific expertise must be evaluated early in research and development because, as with specialists in any industry, experienced professionals in narrowly defined areas can be difficult to find and expensive to hire. Keep in mind that—as with other areas of expertise outside the scientific entrepreneurs' usual skill sets—attracting top-tier talent to a cash-challenged, early-stage company will be challenging. At least initially, it may easier to get comprehensive, experienced talent on an ad-hoc basis. Entrepreneurs must strike a balance between development needs and use of constrained resources on behalf of the company and investor group.

Another source for regulatory talent is the medium-to-large contract research organization (CRO), many of which have regulatory affairs departments. Like independent consultants, CROs balance projects from multiple clients so dedicating resources to a single company may depend on their workload. Entrepreneurs have little influence over contract terms and mandating which CRO employees will be on their project for the duration of development. The decision among these options lies with entrepreneur's comfort level and past experience with a CRO or independent consultant.

BACKGROUND AND EXPERIENCE

Regardless of employment status, the regulatory affairs professional's experience should be the highest consideration for entrepreneurs. A professional with 20+ years of direct strategic and logistical responsibility in industry is considered very experienced. This includes *hands-on* participation in planning and executing regulatory pathways, guiding scientific disciplines involved in the product development process, working with senior executive and management teams, compiling all submission types, and negotiating approvals directly with regulatory agencies. Individuals with this background typically adapt easily and quickly to new regulatory issues if and when they arise.

It may be tempting for company founders to assign regulatory responsibilities to a former colleague with impressive academic credentials or senior ranking in a previous company, but missing hands-on experience. This is often a mistake made when the start-up does not have funding—or is willing to expend some of its limited resources—to hire employees for separate, discreet regulatory tasks. In such cases, it is common for regulatory affairs leadership to "roll up their sleeves" and provide tactical support for the start-up company—so their background must include this experience.

CREDENTIALS

The credentials needed by the well-qualified regulatory affairs professional are frequently debated by personnel in this field. Complicating the matter is that academic degrees and professional certifications vary greatly. A degree in one of the life sciences is extremely helpful, but talented individuals also come from other fields of study. Fundamentally, the regulatory affairs professional should have a strong scientific foundation. A graduate degree in the physical or biomedical sciences provides the needed gravitas to work effectively across development disciplines (which they must do) and for data interpretation. An advanced business degree enables the regulatory affairs professional to clearly understand and accommodate, when possible, the business issues and pressures facing the entrepreneur, investment group, and company.

Several universities now offer master's programs in regulatory affairs. These programs are targeted to new professionals and typically focus on regulatory and product development basics. Curricula include application processes, compliance and quality, advertising and promotion regulations, etc., as well as introductions to clinical development, manufacturing, early stage research, etc. Some programs also include biochemistry, cell biology or other sciences to ensure a foundation for professionals without prior scientific coursework.

Regulatory attorneys can be helpful in cases when a company has compliance issues, reimbursement questions, or lobbying interests which justify legal fees from companies with constrained budgets. However, a legal degree is usually unnecessary for the majority of R&D-based regulatory work faced by a start-up company. Additionally, regulatory attorneys' fees are in line with other legal services, and thus may represent a significant commitment of financial resources. Litigation against regulatory agencies occasionally occurs, is very rarely successful, and is strongly discouraged.

CERTIFICATION

Regulatory affairs certification is offered by several professional societies and academic institutions, and is intended to demonstrate proficiency across most regulatory sub-disciplines in a given country. Credible programs require continuing education to recertify because the regulatory environment is dynamic, and considerable effort is required by a professional to maintain fluency. Many experienced regulatory affairs professional do not have certification, since their extensive experience and academic credentials sufficiently demonstrate proficiency, while new professionals obtain certification to demonstrate competencies in the absence of substantial experience.

CONCLUSIONS

Too often, at their own peril, entrepreneurs pay little heed as to how best to navigate FDA (or related ex-U.S. authorites). Underestimating the importance of regulatory matters is one of the most common mistake entrepreneurs make. A large percentage of early-stage companies fail due to the consequences (e.g., delayed development milestones) of a misguided regulatory path. Do not ignore this key component of your company's growth and development. You would not think of moving forward without devoting some precious, limited funds toward legal assistance (that is the hope, by this point in this book!); the same applies to regulatory assistance. As with the law, entrepreneurs are rarely learned in such matters. Consequently, the regulatory risk of their technologies is too high for investors and other stakeholders—and such parties move on to the next opportunity. When entrepreneurs ask "why can't I get funding/interest?" they usually do not grasp the negative contribution made by a glaring lack of sophistication in this arena.

This chapter offered entrepreneurs and founders a sampling of regulatory issues that should be considered during early- and mid-stage development. Readers will recognize several key themes:

- Most medical products are subject to some level of government regulation, which depends on the level of risk associated with the product or seriousness of the disease in which it is intended to treat
- International regulations, procedures, and statutory framework are country-specific and vary considerably
- Regulatory expertise is critical to success of product development programs, especially when the scope is international and product may have unique medical advantages
- Partnering with experienced regulatory professionals can add important development capabilities to a new company
- Entrepreneurs, founders, and investors should familiarize themselves with regulatory matters that directly or indirectly affect asset value and return on investment

While brevity precluded detailed discussions, entrepreneurs are strongly encouraged to learn as much as possible about the international regulatory landscape their product candidates face.

The goal of every entrepreneur and founder is to streamline product development, maximize the utility of their medical product for patients, and provide expected returns on investment to their funding partners. A firm foundation in regulatory affairs, or access to experienced regulatory partners, will help entrepreneurs achieve this objective.

REFERENCES

1. Devices: General Hospital and Personal Use Devices: Reclassification of Medical Device Data Systems, 73, Fed. Reg. 7498 (proposed 8 Feb 2008)

2. Dietary Supplement and Health Education Act of 1994

3. Conditions Under Which Homeopathic Drugs May Be Marketed, CPG 7132.15, Section 400.400. http://www.fda.gov/ICECI/ComplianceMansuals/CompliancePolicy GuidanceManual/ucm074360.htm

4. The Current State of Global Tissue Regulation. Matthew Weinberg. FDLI Update. November/December 2007, pg. 45

5. Regulating Nanotechnology in the US and EU. Maham Ansari, MS. Regulatory Focus. September 2008, Vol.13, No.9., pgs. 30-34

6. Nanotechnology Task Force Report 2007. Andrew von Eschenbach. U.S. Food and Drug Administration. July 2007. http://www.fda.gov/ScienceResearch/SpecialTopics/Nanotechnology/default.htm

7. A Primer of Drug/Device Law, or What's the Law and How Do I Find It? Josephine C. Babiarz, Esq. in, FDA Regulatory Affairs: A Guide for Prescription Drugs, Medical Devices, and Biologics, Eds. Douglas J. Pisano and David Mantus. CRC Press, 2004

8. Pharmaceutical Administration and Regulations in Japan. Japan Pharmaceutical Manufacturers Association, March 2009, http://www.jpma.or.jp/english/parj/0903.html

9. ICH Global Cooperation Group. Membership list, October 2009. http://www.ich.org/cache/compo/276-254-1.html

10. Simultaneous Global Development; A Case Study: China's Efforts to Address Barriers. S. Wen Chang. Presented at Drug Information Association 45th Annual Meeting, June 2009

11. Guidelines on the Implementation of the WHO Certification Scheme on the Quality of Pharmaceutical Products Moving in International Commerce. www.who.int/medicines/quality_safety/regulation_legislation/certification/guidelines/en/index.html

12. ICH Topic E9: Note for Guidance on Statistical Principles for Clinical Trials. March 1998

13. Surrogate Endpoints in Clinical Trials: are we being mislead? Thomas R. Fleming, PhD, and David L. DeMets, PhD. Annals of Internal Medicine. 1 October 1996. Volume 125, Issue 7, pgs. 605-613

14. Demystifying FDA's 505(b)(2) Drug Registration Process. Harriette L. Nadler, Ph.D., Damaris DeGraft-Johnson, RPh, MSc. Regulatory Focus. October 2009, Vol.14, No.10, pgs 24-30

CHAPTER 9

Roadmap to Reimbursement and Access

Rhonda Greenapple, MSPH
President, Reimbursement Intelligence, LLC

I n 2008, the Federal Drug Administration (FDA) approved 25 novel treatments, an increase from 19 the previous year.[1] However, the cost to bring a drug to market continues to rise along with an increase in the failure rate as products progress through the development process. Currently, there are approximately 2,000 drugs in various stages of clinical development—of which about ¼ are in Phase II/III or Phase III clinical trials. Although the rate of approval improved moderately from 2007 to 2008, the overwhelming majority of pipeline products are never brought to market, as evidenced by the numbers of agents in the pipeline versus those that received FDA approval.[2] Furthermore, the cost of development is an integral component in the selection process of which molecules will be chosen to progress through the development process.[3] The estimated cost of developing a single new chemical entity (NCE) exceeds $800 million, with clinical costs comprising over $400 million of the overall cost. A substantial portion of the development costs is derived from late-stage clinical trials. Given that over 60% of trials are terminated during late-stage development, this is an area of concern for the healthcare industry as a whole due to the resources that are wasted by the failed trials. If pharmaceutical companies were able to terminate 5%

if those Phase III trials that ultimately result in failure, they would realize savings of 5.5-7.1%. Phase III trials are typically the costliest due to the number of patients involved in the trial, often numbering in the thousands, and can cost tens or even hundreds of millions of dollars to conduct. Consequently, even savings of 5.5-7.1% would result in absolute savings of millions of dollars.[4]

This chapter will examine potential strategies and methodologies that product developers and companies can employ in order to maximize the commercial success of their product portfolio. As product developers and manufacturers invest significant resources into development of novel drugs, they must be cognizant of the importance of incorporating the economic value proposition of their pipeline products into the overall value proposition. Currently, the pharmaceutical industry faces significant uncertainty as legislators attempt to address the rising costs of healthcare. Consequently, the economic value proposition may become as important as the clinical profile. Historically, companies focused on the clinical profile of pipeline products and the economic value proposition was often a secondary concern. However, as cost-effectiveness gains traction as one of key components of a drug's value proposition, the companies will have to learn to identify, as well as effectively communicate, their product's economic value story. Most importantly, given the cost of development, the expectations for identification and understanding of a product's economic value story may be earlier in the development process. This chapter will identify the key milestones along the development spectrum as well as offer actionable strategies that will serve to assist the companies in optimizing their product offering's economic value story.[5]

OBJECTIVES

- Know the critical questions to ask regarding access and reimbursement at key product lifecycle milestones
- Identify opportunities and challenges in private and government health plans that can impact commercial success
- Integrate reimbursement and health outcomes activities throughout the commercial planning process

- Ensure continuous monitoring of the entire managed markets landscape that can impact access and reimbursement*

METHODOLOGY

This chapter will review four critical steps in product development: Proof-of-Concept; Opportunity Identification; Pre-launch Planning and; Post-launch and Lifecycle Management. In addition, reimbursement, health outcomes and pricing activities, as well as key questions for consideration at each stage will be identified.

INTRODUCTION

In the current healthcare landscape, there is greater scrutiny paid to expensive biotech products in an environment where biologics represent 30% of the cost of cancer treatment[3] and are evolving into a key component of many therapeutic treatment algorithms. Health plans, both government and private, are attempting to ensure appropriate access and utilization of costly biologics via implementation of management tools such as prior authorization, step edits, quantity limits, and genetic testing. Additionally, a number of public and private health plans have also altered their benefit design to include a specialty tier which often requires the patient to pay a co-insurance for use of injectable and biologic products, with the member paying anywhere from 10-40% of the drug cost.[6]

Health outcomes data becomes even more important for costly biologics, as the Centers for Medicare and Medicaid Services (CMS) and private health plans are considering comparative effectiveness analysis and *lowest cost alternative* when creating their product formularies. In order to maintain access and utilization, companies must be able to demonstrate cost effectiveness and the product's impact on the total cost of care.

---

* According to Webster's New World Dictionary, managed care/markets are defined as "any system that manages healthcare delivery with the aim of controlling costs. Managed care systems typically rely on a primary care physician who acts as a gatekeeper through whom the patient has to go to obtain other health services such as specialty medical care, surgery, or physical therapy." Managed markets include commercial (e.g. HMO, PPO) and government healthcare delivery systems (e.g. Medicare, Medicaid).

Exhibit 1
Share of Enrollment in Medicare Part D Plans with Tiered Cost Sharing Using Specialty Tiers, 2006-2009

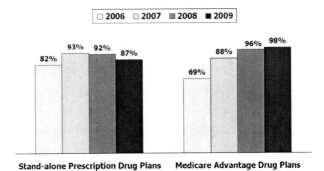

NOTE: Estimates weighted by enrollment in each year.
SOURCE: Georgetown/NORC analysis of data from CMS for MedPAC and the Kaiser Family Foundation.

Exhibit 2
Share of Enrollment in Medicare Part D Plans with Specialty Tiers, by Specialty Tier Coinsurance Rate, 2008-2009

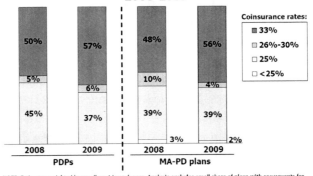

NOTE: Estimates weighted by enrollment in each year. Analysis excludes small share of plans with copayments for specialty tiers (0.1% of PDPs and 2% of MA-PD plans). Analysis of MA-PD plans excludes Special Needs Plans.
SOURCE: Georgetown/NORC analysis of data from CMS for MedPAC and the Kaiser Family Foundation.

Henry J. Kaiser Family Foundation. Medicare Part D Data 2009 Data Spotlight: Specialty Tiers. [Online]. June 2009 [accessed Oct 2 2009]; Available from: URL: http://www.kff.org/

CMS

Medicare and Medicaid programs were originally signed into law in 1965. However, the organizations were not joined together as one entity until 1977. Centers for Medicare and Medicaid Services (CMS) have undergone a number of changes since its formation in the late 1970s, including changes in criteria for inclusion of members in the programs. However, one of the most fundamental changes was made in 2003 with the enactment of the Medicare Modernization Act (MMA). This legislation added an outpatient prescription drug coverage benefit to Medicare, among a number of other integral changes.

Medicare is health insurance that is provided to:
- People over the age of 65
- People under the age of 65 with certain disabilities
- People of all ages with end stage renal disease

Medicare coverage is comprised of four components:
- Part A offers hospital insurance
- Part B covers outpatient medical services and some prescription drugs that are administered by a healthcare professional
- Part C combines Part A and Part B options and must cover all medically necessary services. Part C coverage, also referred to as Medicare Advantage, is offered through private insurance companies that are approved by Medicare
- Part D offers coverage for prescription drugs

Medicaid offers healthcare coverage to certain low-income individuals and families that meet federally and state mandated income thresholds. Medicaid is a state administered program that enables each state to establish their eligibility and policy criteria.

PHASE I: PROOF-OF-CONCEPT

The high cost of product development, coupled with poor economic conditions, makes it vital for entrepreneurs to efficiently and effectively identify products with the greatest potential for commercial success. Conducting a market landscape analysis during early phases of product development helps identify early clinical and economic scenario models that incorporate: (a) the unmet medical needs in the category; (b) the pricing and reimbursement of currently available products and how they are managed; (c) clinical and economic profiles; (d) which health economics outcomes research (HEOR) and clinical endpoints will be required; and (e) ultimately gauge the product's commercial viability.

In oncology, for example, there are more than 850 agents in development.[3] For a new agent in the proof-of-concept stage, the first step will be to determine whether the product can meet an unmet need vs. current or future competitors. In a recent survey regarding key tumor types, Reimbursement Intelligence asked 60 Medical and Pharmacy Directors from private and commercial health plans which tumor types they perceived to have the greatest unmet need for new cancer therapies. The report also assessed the impact of select clinical and HEOR endpoints that novel oncology therapies will be expected to achieve in order to demonstrate incremental value over current standard of care. This type of analysis is the crucial first step in ensuring that resources are allocated appropriately in R&D efforts.

Figure 2. Payers Perception of Unmet Need for New Treatment Options

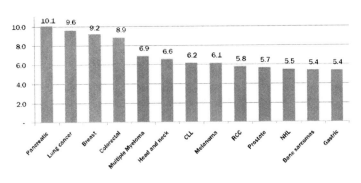

10 = Ranked Greatest Unmet Need,   1 = Ranked Lowest Unmet Need

Another trend in the current healthcare environment is the increase in 505(b)(2) products introduced into the market. As mentioned in Chapter 8, the 505(b)(2) process allows for a faster development time without the need for extensive clinical trials. Generally, 505(b)(2) products are generic products that have new delivery systems, a formulation change, or a novel dosing regimen that allow them to have an abbreviated new drug application (ANDA). The Food and Drug Administration (FDA) allows the companies to use safety and efficacy data already in the public domain, thereby elimi-nating the need to conduct trials that would demonstrate safety and efficacy.[7]

The 505(b)(2) path allows biotech companies to shorten the de-velopment times and significantly lower R&D costs. For example, the migraine product Imitrex (sumatriptan) provides an example of a generic with many iterations introduced under the 505(b)(2) path that utilize novel delivery mechanisms. Below, are three migraine medications that used the 505(b)(2) pathway to launch products de-rived from the same ingredient (sumaptriptan).[7]

Brand	Delivery	Manufacturer
Sumavel™ DosePro™ (su-matriptan injection)	Needle free delivery system	Zogenix
Zelrix™ (sumatriptan transdermal patch)	Transdermal patch	NuPathe®
Levadex™ (sumatriptan oral inhaled)	Oral inhaled	MAP Pharmaceuticals

In these examples, the primary market landscape analysis should focus on the current and future (2 years out) market, including an analysis to determine if payers perceive the new delivery mecha-nism to improved health outcomes—thereby improving the value proposition of the product. With no perceived "value," the 505(b)(2) product will likely be disadvantaged in health plans that have imple-mented generic first formularies designed to transition patients from branded to generic drugs. Conducting comprehensive due diligence at this early stage can help to ensure that the value proposition reso-nates with the appropriate stakeholders.

KEY QUESTIONS FOR CONSIDERATION: "PROOF-OF-CONCEPT"
Does this product meet an unmet need vs. current or future market entrants?
How are payers managing the disease and therapeutic category?
What is the commercial viability?
What HEOR/patient reported outcomes (PRO) has been used in this indication?
What attributes will be important in this category?

PHASE II: OPPORTUNITY IDENTIFICATION

Phase II clinical trials play an integral role in determining the ultimate success or demise of a product. After Phase I trials establish the "proof-of-concept," Phase II trials build upon the outcomes of Phase I trials and further test the molecular entity's safety and efficacy. Furthermore, well-designed and executed Phase II trials should enable the biotech entrepreneur to make the go or no-go decision regarding progression to Phase III trials. Phase III trials often require several years to complete, and can cost tens or even hundreds of millions of dollars. Consequently, companies rely upon the outcomes of Phase II trials to inform and offer guidance for the largest investment they have to make during the development process.[8]

Beyond the associated financial pressures, Phase II trials generally unveil the product's clinical profile, and consequently initiate the development of the compound's value proposition. This early data provides enough information to begin gauging success factors for the product, assuming the trials result in clinical significance. Other market factors, including pricing scenario planning and price sensitivity analysis, economic modeling, value proposition validation and payer evidence requirements, are especially important for companies considering exit strategies for their compound in development. The more information available to support a good market outcome, the more attractive partnerships and acquisitions will be.

Clinical endpoints used in Phase II trials are often mirrored and expanded in Phase III trials. In order to optimize the value proposition of a compound, the company must develop a thorough understanding of the expectations of key stakeholders, including those related to Managed Markets. Although a particular endpoint may be clinically significant, if it does not resonate with managed market key stakeholders, the product could ultimately have market access issues that make it a less desirable compound for development.[9] For example, a company developing a novel therapy for rheumatoid arthritis, which has a costly and crowded existing market, needs to understand how key stakeholders measure efficacy, as well as what their expectations are for most appropriate comparators. Furthermore, the company should seek to understand if the proposed target product profile (TPP) has clinical and economic relevance for payers across all target markets. Although it may seem too early at this phase of development to analyze these market factors, it could ultimately save a manufacturer millions of dollars and thousands of man-hours.

KEY QUESTIONS FOR CONSIDERATION: "OPPORTUNITY IDENTIFICATION"
What PRO endpoints should be included in our clinical trials?
Does the clinical program enhance the value proposition?
Are the endpoints correct comparators, and is the subpopulation in the Phase II studies relevant for market release?
Is there a need to undertake burden of illness studies to support value proposition and market building and positioning activities?
What is the optimal pricing band, based on expected levels of effectiveness, physician & payer perception, and pricing research?

PHASE III: LAUNCH PLANNING AND GLOBAL PRICING AND MARKET ACCESS* (P&MA)

Phase III trials determine how the compound measures up to the current treatment armamentarium. Often called pivotal or comparative trials, Phase III trials involve a large number of patients, and consequently make up the largest portion of drug development costs. It is estimated that 40% of Phase III clinical trials fail.[10] Of those failed trials, 30% fail due to an inability to demonstrate efficacy, while another 30% fail due to toxicity issues, further underscoring the value and importance of Phase II trial design.[11] Although Phase III trials mostly serve in a confirmatory capacity to validate and expand upon the outcomes of earlier phase trials, they ultimately determine the success or failure of a compound.

The outcomes of Phase III trials will be used to construct the compound's clinical and economic value propositions. The company must focus on development of the value proposition which will ultimately influence the pricing, reimbursement, and marketing strate-

* Pricing and Market Access focuses on development and execution of a pricing strategy and the impact of the pricing strategy on the market access of the given product. Pricing and Market Access strategies primarily focus on maximizing the pricing potential of a given products whiles optimizing market access for the product.

gies for the compound. An incorrect or inappropriate selection of comparator(s) or clinical endpoints may lead to irreparable damage to the product's value proposition and, consequently, the product's commercial viability. Similarly, Phase III trials will have a fundamental impact on companies that intend to launch their product in more than one market. Although expectations for outcomes of Phase III trials have a number of similarities—specifically proof of safety and efficacy—a number of differences exist even among neighboring markets. Secondary endpoints, such as quality of life and site of care, can have an integral impact on reimbursement and market access for a product in one market, while having minimal to no impact in other markets. Consequently, companies must be cognizant of the differences in expectations, and factor in those differences in the trial design in order to optimize the value proposition of the compound. To design an effective pricing strategy, the entrepreneur and their executive team must consider all of the nuances and differences in expectation in their clinical trial design.[12]

In considering these variables, it will be important to incorporate vital pre-launch planning activities to uncover and maximize the product's commercial potential. Some critical activities include: (a) development of value messages and global value dossier development; (b) pricing studies and modeling; (c) contracting intelligence, pricing, and reimbursement negotiation tools; (d) global payer segmentation and payer advisory boards; and (e) value drivers.

KEY QUESTIONS FOR CONSIDERATION: "LAUNCH PLANNING & GLOBAL P&MA"
What is the "value" proposition to payers?
What is optimal pricing and reimbursement strategy?
How wide is the price variance across markets?
What is the launch sequence across major markets?
How have we maximized synergy for both US & global markets?
What are the key resources, timelines, and budgets for development of key pricing and reimbursement (P&R), HEOR, and market access milestones?

PHASE IV: POST-LAUNCH AND LIFECYCLE MANAGEMENT

Based on the complexities and the failure rate of gaining approval for a new molecular entity (NME), most companies have allocated significant resources toward expanding the utilization of their marketed compounds. There are several means that companies have at their disposal to maximize and expand the revenues generated by their marketed products. Expanding an indication of a marketed product is one of the most frequently used approaches. In 2004, over 80% of the top selling drugs sought and attained approval for an indication post-launch. The approval of an additional indication enables the manufacturer to gain access to a new market without having to go through the entire development process. While some companies carefully craft their patent extension strategies, others must develop them out of necessity.[13]

A number of companies have launched products which fell short of expectations, or failed to get approval in the targeted indication. Consequently, companies have had to develop a strategy to target another indication and reposition the product. This scenario emphasizes the importance and value of planning and gaining a thorough understanding of the value proposition during the early stages of product development. Pfizer's Viagra™, which originally targeted angina but was most successful as a treatment of erectile dysfunction, is a prime example of a manufacturer repositioning a product in order to maximize sales and extend the life of a drug.[13]

Another approach used by companies to optimize the life and revenue generating capacity of their marketed products is by introducing a new formulation of an existing product. Unlike the addition of a new indication which leverages the product's intrinsic attributes, and consequently is not typically heavily scrutinized, introduction of a novel formulation of an existing product often faces significant scrutiny from payers. Payers are hesitant to pay more for just a novel formulation, unless it offers some concrete benefits, and are specifically looking for improved outcomes.[13]

Another patent life-extending option is the development of a fixed dose combination (FDC) product. Similar to novel formulations of existing products, FDCs using existing or available products can provide a tremendous opportunity and expanded revenue stream, if the product clinical and economic value drivers are relevant to managed market stakeholders. To be effective, an FDC must add incremental value beyond the offering of the individual components. Payers will generally disfavor FDC products that do not offer any incremental value beyond convenience while charging a premium over the individual components. For example, GSK's Advair™ is an FDC that has been far more successful than the individual components that make up the combination. By offering both anti-inflammatory and bronchodialtory activity, Advair was able to offer a distinct advantage which directly translated into improved outcomes, and consequently resulted in preferred access and utilization in most plans.[13]

Conversely, Pfizer's Caduet™, which is a fixed dose combination of two products that will become available in generic form in the near future, has failed to meet expectations. The individual products' (Lipitor™ and Norvasc™) combined sales exceeded $18 billion in 2006, while the FDC attained annual sales of $274 million in 2006. These figures can be attributed directly to a lack of perceived value from a payers perspective. Early analysis of the payer market expectations could have identified these hurdles earlier in development and provided insights as to how the compound could have achieved better payer acceptance. The key stakeholders did not perceive that Caduet™ offered any incremental value over the individual components to warrant a premium price; consequently, the product was disadvantaged in most plans and saw limited uptake.[13]

In this phase, the manufacturer must ensure successful and flawless implementation of the product launch or lifecycle management strategies. These strategies must incorporate communication tactics including: global value slide kits and proposition brochures; payer/HEOR publications; training tools; patient advocacy materials and pull-through activities—as well as health outcomes tactics including: global P&R/HEOR value dossier, cost effectiveness and budget impact models, global database and registry studies, and global pricing research and real world data analysis.

KEY QUESTIONS FOR CONSIDERATION - "POST-LAUNCH & LIFECYCLE MANAGEMENT"
Have we provided clinical, marketing, and account management with consistent (P&MA) messaging and tools?
How are we continuing to differentiate in the market place to maintain and enhance access?
What materials exist to handle P&MA objections?
What impact is the competition placing on pricing & reimbursement?
What are regional/local barriers to market access?
What product changes could trigger new price/reimbursement negotiation or submission?

CONCLUSION

There is a considerable amount of due diligence and analysis that goes into every phase of development for a "successfully" marketed product. Given that costs can exceed $800 million to bring a new drug to market, it is essential to make the commitment to allocate the necessary resources in order to be able to develop a "roadmap" that will identify the impact of market access and pricing factors at each phase of product development. This strategic roadmap increases the likelihood of success throughout the product development process, enabling companies to optimize their investment.

REFERENCES

1. Blum, J. Specialty medicines led rebound in U.S. drug approvals in 2008. Bloomberg [Online] Jan 2009 [cited 2009 Oct 5] Available from: URL: http://www.bloomberg.com

2. David E, Tramontin T, Zemmel R. Pharmaceutical R&D: the road to positive returns. Nat Rev Drug Discov 2009 Aug;8:609-610

3. Medco. 2009 Medco Drug Trend Report [Online]. 2009 [cited 2009 Oct 2]; Available from: URL: http://medco.mediaroom.com

4. Schachter, A. Economic evaluation of Bayesian Model to predict late-phase success of new chemical entities. Value in Health 2007; 10:377-385

5. Nagle, T. Thoughtleader: Thomas Nagle. Pharmaceutical Representative [Online]. May 2007 [cited 2009 Oct 5]; Available from: URL: http://pharmexec.findpharma.com

6. Henry J. Kaiser Family Foundation. Medicare Part D Data 2009 Data Spotlight: Specialty Tiers. [Online]. June 2009 [cited 2009 Oct 2]; Available from: URL: http://www.kff.org/

7. Code of Federal Regulations. Title 21, Volume 5. Revised as of April 1, 2009

8. Chin JY. The clinical side: clinical trials take drugs from the lab to the bedside. Pharmaceutical Representative [Online]. 2004 [cited 2009 Oct 2];[2 screens]. Available from: URL:http://license.icopyright.net/user/viewFreeUse.act?fuid=NTEzMjg3Ng%3D%3D

9. Ratain MJ, Sargent DJ. Optimising the design of phase II oncology trials: the importance of randomization. Eur J Cancer 2009;45:275-280.

10. Collier R. Drug development cost estimates hard to swallow. CMAJ 2009 Feb 3;180(3):279-280

11. Yue C, Colucci P, Ducharme M. Stop costly phase III failures. Applied Clinical Trials [serial on the Internet]. (2009, June), [cited 2009 Oct 2];18(6):4-6. Available from: Academic Search Premier

12. Optimal launch sequence for pharmaceuticals within the EU. M.C. Gouy Consulting GmbH 2000 May:1-6

13. Sandner P, Ziegelbauer K. Product-related research: how research can contribute to successful life-cycle management. Drug Discov Today 2008 May;13(9/10):457-463

CHAPTER 10

Working Toward a Successful Exit

James Hawkins, PhD, MBA
Managing Director, FOCUS Securities, LLC

This chapter is intended to touch on some of the significant matters involved in building value into, and realizing a monetary return on (or "exiting"), a biotechnology venture. It is not intended to be a comprehensive "How To" manual on these topics. However, these discussions can allow a reader to anticipate, thoughtfully react to, and periodically reflect back upon subjects that mark a company's development, and that condition the exit of investors from a biotechnology company.

Starting a biotechnology company is probably one of the most exhilarating and adventuresome efforts that can be undertaken in our society. It is also one of the most difficult and daunting. It is exciting because it presents the possibility of having a positive effect on people's lives through the development of new medical products; it also offers the possibility of substantial monetary reward. It is daunting because a biotechnology company is one of the riskiest, fastest moving, and most rapidly changing enterprises. For all of these reasons, the management of stakeholders' expectation is invariably complex.

Notwithstanding the challenge, once value has been built into a biotechnology enterprise, how do stakeholders get rewarded for their efforts? How do they realize an investment "exit?" The topic of the exit of shareholders from a biotechnology company is the focus of this chapter.

WHO STARTS BIOTECHNOLOGY COMPANIES? AN OVERVIEW

Most biotechnology companies start out in one of three ways. Most often, a research scientist has an idea—often a technical idea with no immediate market application. This usually happens when the scientist is familiar with a specific technology or a new and emerging area of scientific discovery. Less often, an individual who has had considerable middle management experience in a large company sees an opportunity—often a more mature market opportunity—and decides to go out on their own and attempt to exploit it. Least often, two people join forces: an experienced entrepreneur or senior manager, who has built and successfully exited a biotechnology company, teams with an experienced financial backer, who has backed and successfully exited one or more biotechnology companies. Together, they carefully select a project or existing company on which to work.

For the purpose of this chapter, we will focus on the first type of founder: the research scientist. This stated, all three types of founders—the research scientist, the experienced middle manager, and the professional investment team—will find value in this discussion. This chapter may also provide insights for other stakeholders who need to work with and understand the scientific founder in order to build value into a biotechnology company, and provide for a successful exit to all shareholders.

WHAT IS A SUCCESSFUL EXIT?

In strict terms, a successful exit from a company is one in which the individuals who own stock in the company realize a greater amount of money than their original investment, when their stock is finally sold. The greater the return, the better; the shorter the time to exit, the better. In all cases, the most successful exit is one where the investors maximize the return on investment or realize their preferred level of return over their preferred period for investment.

What are the basic metrics of a successful exit from a biotechnology investment? It would be fair to say that a venture capitalist—the investor requiring the most aggressive return on a biotechnology investment—would like to realize significant (sometimes as much as 50-100-fold) return on their investment within a couple of years. However, a return of ten times the original amount invested, received after 5 years, would be considered by a venture capitalist—and, hence, by most other types of investors—as a very desirable and successful exit from a start-up biotechnology company.

The important thing to bear in mind is that the return on different investment opportunities will be quantitatively and qualitatively different, depending on the basic nature and fortunes of the particular biotechnology company. However, an exit will be successful when the company has been able to maximize the return on investment to the maximum number of shareholders whatever the circumstances.

BUILDING VALUE INTO A BIOTECHNOLOGY INVESTMENT?

The value of a biotechnology company is unpredictable until exit. It can grow steadily or it fluctuate several times—from almost nothing to an unrealistically inflated value—before any shareholder can realize a return on investment. This situation exists because the value of a biotechnology company is the function of two components. First, it is a function of the inherent objective value of a company's product class as a business proposition. Second, it is a function of a more subjective, perceived value of the company relative to the mood and fashion of the financial markets.

THE OBJECTIVE VALUE OF A BIOTECHNOLOGY COMPANY: DEFINED BY COMPANY PRODUCT TYPE

There are four basic types of biotechnology products: 1) research products, 2) research instruments, 3) clinical diagnostics and medical devices, and 4) pharmaceuticals. The value of a basic type of biotechnology product—and the relative value of a biotechnology company developing this type of product—is related to seven characteristics listed in Table 1. Generally, the longer the development time and the greater the development risk, the more valuable the product/company will be. Similarly, if a company's product requires approval by a regulatory agency or requires intellectual property protection,

Table 1: Characteristics of biotechnology products and their relationships to the relative business value of biotechnology companies. "+" indicates some correlation, "+++++" indicates greatest correlation.

	Research products	Research instruments	Diagnostics, devices	Drugs and biologics
Length of product development cycle	+	++	++	++++
Product development risk	+	++	+++	+++++
Regulatory requirements			++	+++++
Intellectual property		+	+++	+++++
Capital need	+	++	+++	+++++
Opportunity for organic growth	+++++	+	+	
Need for professional management		+	++	++++
Relative value of company at exit	least	second least	second most	most

the higher the eventual value of the product/company. If a product requires a large amount of capital to be developed, and this capital cannot be obtained through organic growth of the company's revenues/profits, then the product will increase in value because of the need for outside financing. Finally, companies that develop increasingly valuable products require increasingly sophisticated management teams. Table 1 summarizes the characteristics needed for the development of different types of biotechnology products. The relative value at exit of companies successfully developing each of these types of products is also illustrated. This value is derived from accepted norms of business and reflects a relatively objective value of the company.

THE SUBJECTIVE VALUE OF A BIOTECHNOLOGY COMPANY

Almost anything can happen to the value of a biotechnology company before final development of a biotechnology product has been reached and a market established for that product. For example, the company may be involved in a "hot" technology that strategic investors want to capitalize on, resulting in an inflated value of the company. On the other hand, a particular technology, like gene therapy, may have a clinical setback, arbitrarily dropping the value of all companies in the same field. The company may also have a promising story but run out of money before it can fully develop its product, resulting in no return on investment at all.

Generally speaking, the subjective value of a company is not a function of business criteria. It is largely a function of financial criteria that often relate to the ability of a company to carry out a transaction at some point in a product development cycle before the product is completed.

VALUE OF A BIOTECHNOLOGY COMPANY AS A FUNCTION OF PRODUCT DEVELOPMENT CYCLE

The relative value of a biotechnology company over time can be measured by milestones that the company achieves. Subjective milestones must be used to assess increasing value in most early biotechnology companies, before more objective monetary measures such as revenues and profits come in to play. One type of milestone, "scientific proof-of-principle," must be achieved for any new technology. For example, the scientific milestone for a new type of antibiotic would be the demonstration that the antibiotic compound can kill bacteria in a test tube. This type of demonstration can raise the value of a company. Another, more advanced, scientific milestone would be the demonstration that the antibiotic can kill bacteria in human subjects. This could be achieved through staged approval and testing of the compound in conjunction with a government regulatory agency, such as the U.S. Food and Drug Administration (FDA).

Finally, an approved product must demonstrate its ability to achieve commercial milestones. It must be able to find application in different types of commercial markets and to compete effectively with other products in these markets. That is, it must achieve "commercial proof-of-principle." The further a product moves along the pathway to commercial development, the more a company can be measured in monetary terms. For example, the ability of a company to generate revenues from product sales is a significant milestone;

the ability to generate profits is the final test of a new biotechnology product and company.

Running the gauntlet of building value for a biotech product and company can be analogized to a game of baseball. The result from any inning in a baseball game can be very good or very bad for your team; the team's score can fluctuate relative to an opponent's. The result of the game is only determined after the tally of all innings is taken. Similarly, it is only after effort is expended on establishing scientific and commercial proof-of-principle that the final value of a biotechnology product and the ultimate value of a biotechnology company can be objectively determined. To complete the analogy, it must be noted that a biotechnology company seldom achieves value or an exit if it runs out of money at any point in its development; there is no winner in a baseball game if the game is called on account of rain.

At the end of a full and successful product development cycle, the exit for investors from a biotechnology company is relatively straightforward. In addition, the approximate return for an investor can be predicted with considerable objectivity and some certainty. However, until that point, it is a combination of objective and subjective features of a company's product that determine the moment-to-moment value of a biotechnology company.

CHALLENGES TO BUILDING COMPANY VALUE: OPPORTUNISM AND BAD BEHAVIOR

Inherent uncertainties in the perceived value of a biotechnology company, before it achieves full product development, may lead to considerable opportunism among different groups or shareholders and other stakeholders. Because of the inherent variability of value in a biotechnology company, described above, later investors may be able to gain advantages over earlier investors money is raised to continue funding operations. All investors will experience a proportionate decrease or "dilution" in the relative number of shares they own after any funding round. Nonetheless, the earlier an investor holds shares in a company, the greater the chance that he/she will experience disproportionate "dilution" of his/her shares in a "down round" where the company's value is perceived to be lower than expected. In this regard, it is not unusual to hear stories of founders of biotechnology companies whose equity position in a company has been diluted to such an extent by covenants in the shareholder agreements of later investors that his/her return on exit is *de minimis*.

How can one guard against the inherent uncertainty of long product development cycles and possible opportunism of fellow investors in order to maximize the chance for a successful exit from a biotechnology company? This can be done in two ways: first, know your fellow shareholders; second, know your stakeholders.

KNOW YOUR SHAREHOLDERS

There are basically five types of shareholders who invest in biotechnology companies:

1. Founder(s)
2. Individuals with a personal relationship to founder(s) (often family and friends of the founder)
3. High net worth individuals, often referred to as "angel" investors
4. Institutional investors who manage investment funds and invest other people's money (most often venture capitalists)
5. The public, through public markets
6. Each of these investor groups and their own particular needs must be considered from the inception of a biotechnology company until the exit of each investor. Each of these investor groups and some of their unique characteristics are discussed below and outlined in Table 2.

TYPES OF SHAREHOLDERS: FOUNDERS

Founders of biotechnology companies are the entrepreneurs of science. They often possess a unique understanding of a particular technology or subject of science at a level where they are indispensable to the company for some period of time, until this knowledge is transferred into the hands of others. A founder is accorded a particular amount of stock in the company at its inception. This stock allocation is to recognize the fact that a founder is taking a risk starting a speculative venture, and that they will contribute time, effort, and a unique talent to the enterprise,

Table 2: Different types of investors in biotechnology companies and the general characteristics for each of these investment groups

Investor group	Range of total cash investment	Level of investment experience	Ability to provide additional "follow-on" investment	Point of investment; investment horizon
Founder(s)	up to $50,000	Limited	very limited	years 0–3; 10 years
Family and friends	up to $50,000	Limited	limited	year 1–3; up to 10 years
High net worth or "angel" investors	from $50,000 to $250,000	moderate	moderate	year 1–4; 5 to 10 years
Institutional investors	from $250,000 to $20 million	sophisticated	strong and planned	year 1–7; 5 to 10 years
Public markets	above $80 million	limited to sophisticated	strong if company is successful	year 7 onward; days to years

All Stock is Not Perceived as Equal

The stock a founder receives at the beginning of a company is often colloquially termed "founder's stock." This terminology is not because it is legally any different from other stock issued by the company; it is usually "common" stock like that of most other early investors. However, this stock is usually issued for a nominal price: a few cents to a few dollars per share. The fact that a founder receives so much stock and pays so little money for it is often a silent bone of contention as a company grows and new investors with different perspectives become co-investors. Why?

At first, the distribution of stock to founders seems fair because most people intuitively accept that reward is proportional to risk. A founder takes the ultimate risk in starting a company, and therefore should be rewarded amply in stock. However, most people will also accept that it is not the amount of stock that you own in a company—but the amount of money that you have actually invested that determines your most basic level of commitment to the company. It is a positive attribute to investors that founders have risked some of their own funds to the start-up; what is known as "skin in the game." Moreover, most people feel more committed to other people who are risking "cash money" in an investment rather than those contributing little or no money and "only" their efforts. This is also why the stock or "equity" that a founder owns is referred to as "sweat equity."

In a perfect world, the perception of "two classes of stock"—founder's and other investor's stock—should not take place in a company. This notion is reinforced by the fact that with each new round of investment, a founder is "diluted" in his/her stock position in the same manner as other investors. ("Diluted" refers to someone [*e.g.*, a founder] owning a lower and lower percentage of the company. As more stock is distributed, their number of shares remains unchanged.) However, there is an inflection point in the development of every company where cash money is seen as superior to sweat equity, and proportionate dilution does not seem to make up the difference. This situation can lead to conflict between a founder and later investors. To some more unscrupulous, later investors, the solution to this perceived inequity is often to construct a pretense to disproportionately diminish the founder's stock position in order to assuage the later investor's perceived disparity (on the high side) in company ownership.

What can a founder do to prevent or minimize discord with other, non-founder, later investors? One solution is to insist upon drawing a proper salary as new groups of investors enter the company and company milestones are achieved. The emphasis here is on "proper" salary; this would be a salary that a non-founder individual doing a similar job in a comparable company would draw. Often, entrepreneurs think of the company they formed as "their" company; one in which they can set their own compensation. It is worth noting that the moment founders accept money from investors, it is no longer "their" company. In this regard, a founder no longer has the prerogative to set his/her own salary like a sole proprietor. By the same token, an investor should be expected to pay a proper salary to all employees of a company—including the founder(s).

Once receiving a proper salary, a founder is well advised to invest a considerable proportion of this salary back into the company. In this way, a founder can credibly contend that he is continuing in his commitment to the company by investing the same "cash money" as other later investors. That is, maintaining a sharing of risk by continuing to have "skin in the game." Parenthetically, by investing money in the firm, the founder will also gain a more realistic perspective on what other investors are feeling when money is spent inside the company, or more money is needed to advance the company's growth. In short, one is more sensitized when one has to write a check for something.

Additionally, this commitment is also useful when it comes to matters of debt. Very often, a startup company is short of cash until new financing arrives. In this situation the founder is often asked to go without part or all of his/her salary. Unfortunately, when new investors come into a company, they are not anxious to repay deferred salary and the founder is asked to write off this income. There is actually an understandable perspective on the part of the new investor—he/she wants to invest in the future of the company, not in its past. However, if the founder defers salary payments this should always be recorded as debt and it is appropriate that this founder debt and the debt of existing investors be treated in the same fashion if demands are made for debt conversion by new investors. Fair is fair.

It is imperative in establishing the position of a founder in a company that the founder has an experienced lawyer involved from the very beginning, to set up the company and establish appropriate legal documents for all shareholders. Moreover, a business attorney should be consulted regularly as the biotechnology company changes over time and new shareholders are brought into the enterprise.

TYPES OF SHAREHOLDERS: INDIVIDUALS WITH A PERSONAL RELATIONSHIP WITH THE FOUNDER

After the founder, the first investors in a company are likely individuals who have a personal relationship with the founder. They are motivated to invest in the company out of a feeling of friendship or obligation to the founder. They usually comprise the founder's family or close friends. Many of these individuals are not experienced or sophisticated in making high risk investments. For these reasons, it is important that each investor be formally qualified as an investor under an appropriate exemption in the securities law. Again, an experienced business lawyer can draw up the appropriate documents.

When accepting investments from friends, the impact that the outcome of the investment may have on a founder's relationship with a relative or friend may be more important than conforming to the letter of the law. It can almost be assured that if an investment goes well, and everybody exits with more than their original investment, everybody will be happy. However, since more biotechnology companies fail than succeed, it is very important to consider the impact on personal relationships if the company fails.

Some rules of thumb apply to investments from friends and relatives. First, never take an investment that the investor cannot afford to lose or an investment that will cause the investor to make major sacrifices or change their lifestyle. Generally, most unsophisticated investors become increasingly uncomfortable investing sums above $10,000. No individual—irrespective of how much money they have—likes to lose more than $50,000. Another point that needs to be made strongly to unsophisticated investors is that even if the company does well, it is very difficult to exit an investment in a private company at any time—even if the investor just wants their money back with no return. The situation common to most types of investments, where lack of liquidity is off-set by higher returns and less risk, is not the case here. Thus, it should be pointed out to an investor that their money is locked up until a "liquidity event" takes place, finally allowing all investors to share in a cash return on their investment. Moreover, most exits take place years from the point where family and friends are likely to invest in an early-stage biotechnology enterprise.

Finally, a founder should bear in mind that they are subjecting every investor to two types of risk. First, an investor is subjected to the inherent business risk associated with a rapidly growing, early-stage company. However, every investor is also subject to the risk of dishonest dealings in a company as new individuals become associated with the firm. It is one thing for an investor to lose money through taking a known risk; most investors will accept an "honest loss." But, it is quite another thing if people lose their money in a situation where they are disadvantaged by unscrupulous dealings by someone other than the founder. In such cases, an investor may blame a founder … and a founder may blame him or herself for leading a close friend or family member into the company that later took on untrustworthy or narrowly self-interested people who felt no personal responsibility to provide a fair and proportionate exit for the founder's family and friends.

HIGH NET WORTH INDIVIDUALS; "ANGEL" INVESTORS

High net worth individuals can form a very important part of the "capital structure" or financing strategy of an early-stage company. In general, angel investors can provide larger investments than family and friends. However, most angel investors cannot supply additional investment or "follow-on" to a significant extent once their initial investment has been made.

A good founder should be cognizant that an angel investor likely has mixed motives for investing. As with other investors, an angel investor would like to receive a return on investment—this must never be forgotten. However, it is often noted that angel investors also have further "psychological" motivations for investment. For example, in biotechnology, an angel investor may be motivated to invest in a company that is working in a disease area that has affected someone they hold dear. An angel may invest in an entrepreneur because he identifies with, and wants to help, someone who has taken risk—or who may even be following the path that the investor took to become successful. In general, angel investors have become more sophisticated over time. Still, less experienced angel investors may agree to company valuations or terms of investment that may not be acceptable to later institutional investors. Moreover, the more investors that are brought into a company, the more complex each round of funding becomes.

Finally, angel investors are often a source of good advice to early entrepreneurs. On the other hand, the angel investor who starts to get actively involved in the management of the company, or feels that their investment gives them prerogative to run the company, is overstepping their proper role as an investor and may not be perceived well by other investors or company staff.

INSTITUTIONAL INVESTORS

Institutional investors come in three varieties: venture capital groups, private equity groups, and hedge funds. In general, venture capital firms deal with companies that are pre-revenue having less experienced or smaller management teams; that is, the majority of biotechnology companies. Private equity groups deal almost exclusively with more mature revenue- and profit-generating companies that have a full complement of professional managers. Hedge funds deal with very special situations in the financing of both early-stage and later stage biotechnology companies; for example, in alternative public financings discussed below.

Institutional investors are very different from the first three categories of investor discussed, because of the way they raise and invest money. Venture capital, private equity groups, and hedge funds raise the majority of their funds from other entities such as high net worth families or "family offices," pension funds, or large corporations. In this regard, institutional investors use "other people's money." Institutional investors take the pool of money they raise and combine it into a specific fund. This fund has certain criteria for investment related to the type of industry that money will be invested in; for example, biotechnology and pharmaceuticals. Generally, the smaller the fund, the fewer types of fields will be the subject of investment. To mitigate risk, a fund will also develop criteria regarding the concentration of investment in any given company; few funds will invest more than 10% of the fund in any given company. In order to further spread risk yet still make large investments, many institutional investors will bring other institutional investors into an opportunity as co-investors. Finally, a fund will also have certain expectations for return on investment to fund investors. For the most part, an investment fund will expect to have all of the fund's capital invested within about 2-3 years, and expect to exit investments in 3-7 years.

The nature and dynamics of fund structure peculiar to an institutional investor type of investment has several consequences for the biotechnology company. First, institutional investors have a great deal more money than most other types of investors; they have so-called "deep pockets." For this reason, they can fund biotechnology companies requiring large amounts of money that other investors do not have; for example, companies developing therapeutic products requiring a series of clinical trials. In this regard, institutional investors can place multiple rounds of capital in a company they want to continually support—also known as "follow-on" Investment.

Most importantly, institutional investors are "portfolio managers." This means a strategy of investing their funds across a number of companies and technology/market sectors so as to initially spread their risk. But, over time, they also want to limit their investment to only the companies that are going to maximize the return for their portfolio. Because of this strategy, a biotechnology company is, in effect, in competition with the other companies in an institutional investor's portfolio. For this reason, an institutional investor's motives and rationale for investment are theoretically the most objective and practical of all investors.

In addition, it should be mentioned that the institutional investor will come with investment terms that may seem draconian; very much investor-friendly rather than company-friendly. Inevitably, most of these terms will need to be accepted by early investors due to their continual and urgent capital requirements. For this reason, if the fortunes of a biotechnology company turn sour at some point— even if they improve later—early investors may be significantly diluted by institutional investment.

THE PUBLIC

Early-stage companies are often precluded from offering securities directly to the public. In fact, it is only under certain special provisions in the securities laws that families, friends and angel investors can be offered securities. In general, securities must be registered with the government before they can be sold to the public at large. On the other hand, institutional investors and large corporate entities are considered sophisticated investors who are knowledgeable in investment matters; they can be approached directly for investment in a biotechnology company. Most institutional investors who invest in biotechnology prefer to have their first investments in a private company. As the company matures, the institutional investor can realize a premium on their investment if the private biotechnology company "goes public."

Because of securities laws, stock in a company is usually sold to the public at a much later stage in the company's growth. Moreover, a company usually receives funding from most other types of investors before it begins to take investments from the public. While offering stock to the public provides a company with a broader base of funding, it also creates a whole new level of responsibility and expense. For example, a public company must regularly file financial reports to regulatory authorities—such as the Securities and Exchange Commission. This reporting function is very expensive. These reports are also available publicly to everyone, including the company's competitors.

KNOW YOUR STAKEHOLDERS

In addition to the shareholders of a company who contribute capital, other groups of people and institutions contribute to the value of a biotechnology company through services they provide to a company. Perhaps one of the best methods to ensure that investors maximize the return on their investment is to make sure that each stakeholder group is well enfranchised in the company and that the needs of each of the stakeholder groups is defined and addressed on an ongoing basis.

SO WHO ARE THE STAKEHOLDERS IN A BIOTECHNOLOGY BUSINESS?

There are many stakeholders in an early-stage biotechnology enterprise. These individuals or institutions may not be obvious on day one, But within the first year of a company's founding, they should all be starting to come on to the radar screen of any new company that is positioning itself properly in the biotechnology community. From the perspective of headcount, most stakeholders are evident in a company as it employs 10 to 20 employees.

Obvious stakeholders include: employees, members of the board of directors, and outside professional advisors such as lawyers and accountants. Other less-obvious stakeholders include: customers, vendors, and even the government—in various incarnations from local government to federal regulatory bodies and tax authorities.

Even industry competitors should be thought of as stakeholders. Other, even less obvious groups (*e.g.*, potential strategic partners or acquirers) are potential stakeholders whose future role will be to provide an exit for investors.

The state of mind of stakeholders, and the ability of these individuals and institutions to achieve their own objectives during the growth of the biotechnology company, is often directly related to the greater success of a company. Stakeholders often play a critical role in how a company's reputation in the life science and local business community is built. A company that treats employees badly will stop attracting the best employees. A company who cannot work well with professional advisors will not gain access to the valuable networks these advisors can access on its behalf. The perspective of stakeholders may ultimately determine a company's ability to maximize the value of the firm, as well as achieve the best the exit for investors.

PROFESSIONAL ADVISORS

Different stakeholders perform different functions at different times during the company's growth. Professional advisors likely have the greatest effect on conditioning and finally executing on the exit for investors. For example, legal advisors can provide the legal foundation and documentation of investments, contracts, and other business that the company undertakes during its growth. Accountants provide the essential record of a company's day-to-day financial activities, in addition to the periodic reports that are necessary for future investment and exit for investors. Finally, the investment banker is the driving force that will undertake the transaction that will ultimately allow investors to exit and maximize their return on investment. All these advisors should be cultivated early in a company's existence and consulted as each new milestone of company value is reached.

HOW TO EXIT A BIOTECHNOLOGY COMPANY: IMPORTANT PERSPECTIVES RELATED TO THE EXIT

PERSPECTIVE OF A SCIENTIFIC FOUNDER

In some ways, the research scientist (or similar person upon which the company's technology is based) is least prepared to undertake a start-up company, manage its growth, and engineer an exit for shareholders. This is because most scientists build their perceptions of a company around their long experience in academic institutions. In essence, academia is perhaps the worst model of an organization for a scientific entrepreneur to analogize to the operation of a small and growing commercial enterprise like a biotechnology company.

Why? Overall, academic institutions provide little credit or value to commercial enterprises. For the most part, scientists are taught to value intellect and publication of experimental results far above the development of practical products and the use of money. Further, it stifles the entrepreneurial spirit when factors such as patents are non-factors in the tenure-track process. For example, there ends up being more interest in serving on graduate studies committees than in clinical or applied research. For these reasons, academic training often gives a scientist an inflated value of his/her contribution to a commercial enterprise—and a discounted value to those who provide capital or management skills to an enterprise with the objective of product development and commercialization.

These skewed perceptions of business and finance are also reinforced by the way scientists are supported and rewarded in academic institutions. Scientists are supported by research grants that never need to be repaid in cash money. This makes the basic premise of the role of financial stakeholders very abstract to scientists. The scientist ends up more likely to think that the financial stakeholder owes them support because of their scientific credentials and brilliant ideas. Instead, the scientist should think that they are developing a greater and greater obligation to repay and find an exit for the financial investor through the science and product development that is being carried out in a company.

Finally, the consequence of failure in business is not often concrete to a scientific founder. In academia, scientists do not lose their jobs if their experiments do not work out. In stark contrast, a small business—where it is commonplace for biotechnology companies to run with less than one year of funding—may immediately and permanently close if business milestones are not met.

JUST BECAUSE YOU'RE PARANOID DOESN'T MEAN THEY'RE NOT OUT TO GET YOU

Scientists often have difficulty adapting to an early-stage commercial environment. But the problem is not one-sided. Those who deal with scientists are also often guilty of not educating scientific partners, or do not enfranchise the scientist in management discussions and decisions. There are many examples of scientists who have founded and built companies, only to find that as soon as a company becomes valuable, their authority in company operations is reduced without objective consideration, and their ownership position is disproportionately diluted.

ADVICE TO SCIENTIFIC FOUNDERS ABOUT SHAREHOLDERS

The best advice to scientific founders is to get to know your shareholders personally, and try to understand their motives for involvement in your business. It is important to communicate regularly with fellow shareholders, and to listen to their opinions, needs, and expectations. In addition, it is important for a founder to understand how shareholders feel about their involvement in the company at any given time.

The job of an entrepreneurial founder is always busy. There is temptation to focus on the many competing matters at hand, and avoid the discipline of regular communications with shareholders and stakeholders. However, a founder does this at his peril. It takes a lot less time to stay in touch with people and anticipate a problem— or nip one in the bud—than it does to have an avoidable problem explode unpredictably, becoming a major distraction that consumes inordinate amounts of time and emotional energy.

The point at which a scientific founder begins to mature and the probability of a company's success increases significantly is when their perspective begins to shift from, "what do I want from my shareholders?" to "what do my shareholders need from me?"

HOW MUCH OF A BIOTECHNOLOGY COMPANY SHOULD THE SCIENTIFIC FOUNDER(S) OWN AT EXIT?

Many founders feel that they should always own a majority of their company. This is possible if the company is a scientific services company like a clinical research organization (CRO) or a company that provides simple scientific products, such as reagents or consumables. However, the growth of a typical biotechnology company developing new technologies is carried out in stages. At the beginning, before scientific proof-of-principle/concept is established, a scientific founder could well own a majority of the company. Often, by the time scientific proof-of-principle is established, the founder will own less than a majority. A founder will be further diluted as commercial proof-of-principle is established. Assuming that a technology succeeds and shows commercial promise, a founder will likely own 5% or less of a company by exit.

To some entrepreneurs, the notion of giving up ownership of a company is disconcerting. However, as a generalization, the development of any product that requires regulatory approval and a lengthy path to commercialization requires a quantity of capital and a rate of capital expenditure (i.e., "burn rate"). In turn, this reality necessitates raising significant amounts of capital (usually equity investment). The result of serial rounds of investment is the dilution of a founder to a minority position. The analogy often used to explain the non-intuitive dynamic of greater dilution leading to greater value at exit is as follows: although the piece of "value pie" the founder is receiving is progressively smaller, the pie itself is getting much bigger, so the founder is netting an increasing amount of pie. Stated another way, the founder is getting a smaller share of a larger return, and this value will ultimately surpass a bigger share of a much smaller return.

THE MECHANICS OF EXITING A BIOTECHNOLOGY COMPANY

There are several ways for investors to exit a biotechnology company investment. The two major routes include: (1) sale of the company, or (2) licensing of the assets of the company. Sale of the company usually provides an immediate or rapid cash payout to investors from the buyer. Licensing the assets of a company usually results in payout to investors over time. Variations on these two basic methods of exiting a company are outlined in Table 3, and detailed further below.

EXIT THROUGH SALE OF THE BIOTECHNOLOGY COMPANY

Once a biotechnology company has achieved objective milestones, its value will rise. At some point, this value will be considered sufficient for sale of the company to an interested buyer. At that time, it will be important for shareholders to retain an investment banker to advise on and manage the sale of the company. The investment banker will either sell the company privately or create a public market for the stock of the company. If the company is sold privately, the founder and other investors will receive a return directly from the buyer. If the company is taken public, investors can then sell their stock in the public market and receive a return in this manner. The dynamics of these two approaches to shareholder exit are discussed further below.

PRIVATE SALE OF THE COMPANY

There are two basic types of buyers who participate in the private sale of a company: strategic and financial. A strategic buyer is likely to be another larger biotechnology company that wants to: 1) acquire a new company in order to grow more rapidly in size, 2) obtain a product or technology that complements the buyer's basic business, or 3) both. In any case, because the acquisition is strategic, the price paid is likely to be at a premium. In this regard, return on investment is usually maximized through a sale to a strategic buyer as opposed to a financial buyer. Furthermore, because a strategic buyer already has a company infrastructure, the strategic buyer will often be prepared to buy all of the company at once—allowing founders and other investors to cash out immediately.

Table 3: Characteristics of different routes available for investors in biotechnology companies to exit and receive a return on investment

Type of exit	Amount of stock sold over time	Return on investment	Risk against maximum return
Private sale of stock to strategic buyer	all at once	maximum for one transaction	low
Private sale of stock to financial buyer	all at once or two-part sale over time	high; likely higher with two-part transaction	low to moderate
Sale of stock to the public	all at once or any amounts over time	variable	moderate
Licensing of property in exchange for ongoing royalties	none	maximum over time	moderate

The typical financial buyer of a company is the private equity group. At the time of purchase, this buyer will usually cash out all past investors. Still, they may want the founder to continue to work for the company. They may also want the founder to maintain ownership of some or a majority of the stock—until the company has transitioned to the control of the new buyer/investor, or reached a new value point through the achievement of certain milestones. In this case, the founder may not realize his full return on investment for some period of time. On the other hand, a financial buyer will eventually want to acquire all of the company and exit the investment themselves. In this case, a founder stands the chance of getting "two bites from the apple." That is to say, the founder achieves an initial exit when the financial buyer acquires part of the company along some of the founder's equity—the first bite. A second bite is achieved when the buyer acquires the remainder of the company including the founders' remaining stock, or sells the company in conjunction with the founder selling his stock to a new acquirer. In either case, the founder is likely to get a premium for their second sale of equity.

With regard to practical matters, it usually takes an investment bank about 6 months to identify either strategic or financial buyers, contact these potential buyers, and conduct an auction to maximize the price for the company and return for investors.

Exit Through Creating a Public Company

Investors can also exit a company if it "goes public;" that is, if a public market is created for the company's stock. Large companies needing to raise in excess of $50-80 million can undertake an initial public offering or "IPO." Once the stock of the company can be traded in a stock market, any person holding unrestricted stock in the company can sell their stock and realize a return on their initial investment.

From a practical standpoint, IPOs are time-consuming. Also, it is never certain that a robust market in the company's stock will be established immediately that will allow an investor to sell all of their stock right away, or at a consistently attractive price. For these reasons, return on investment is variable depending on the fortunes of a company's stock.

A variation on the full IPO process can also allow smaller biotechnology companies to take their firms public. This process is referred to as "alternative public financing." For a private company, this entails the reverse merger of the private biotechnology company with a public "shell" corporation. In this merger, a new public entity is created. This merger can be done in conjunction with the discounted sale of company stock to institutional investors. This accomplishes two things. First, it provides the company with immediate capital. Second, it creates a public market for the stock of all investors. It is important to note that some in the financial community view reverse mergers as the joining of two weaklings: combining an already-public firm in distress with a private company unable to IPO on its own.

OTHER EXITS FOR INVESTORS

During the life of a biotechnology company, a particular product or technology within the company may achieve value unto itself. If the company does not want to wait to begin to gain a return from this technology through the sale of the company, this value can be realized early through the licensing of the technology to an interested party. As royalties are paid by the licensee to the licensor, this income may be distributed to investors. Over time, this return may be appreciable and will be paid independent of the performance of the company.

SUMMARY

Most biotechnology companies work with new technologies. It is often difficult to predict if and when these technologies will result in valuable products, and if the company developing these products will become valuable itself, bringing a return on investment to investors.

Notwithstanding the risk associated with developing value into a biotechnology company, there are several ways for an investor to exit a biotechnology enterprise once value has been established. First, a biotechnology company can be sold privately to either a strategic or financial buyer. Alternatively, a company may license its technology and direct these royalty fees to investors. Finally, biotechnology companies can construct exits for investors in public markets through undertaking a traditional IPO or an alternative public financing strategy.

CHAPTER 11

Effective Networking

Susan K. Finston
President, Finston Consulting, LLC

S ome people appear to have the knack of meeting just the right person at the just the right time, and to effortlessly gain access to financing and technical support for the growth and development of their entrepreneurial efforts. Are these people just lucky—or is there something else at work?

In fact, what may look superficially like luck is actually the result of focused and consistent effort to develop the right contacts and leads. Much more often, knowing the right contact for a particular situation is the outcome of hard work and investment in effective networking, as well as other long-term efforts. In general, networking is a means to an end—not an end in itself—and can be used to expand contacts to make the most of scarce resources (time, money, staff, etc.), either before launch of a start-up or in the early phases.

As Samuel Goldwyn famously said, "The harder I work, the luckier I get." The purpose of this chapter is to outline ways to improve your odds; i.e., to help you to "get lucky" through effective networking. This may not come easily, but by working systematically and persistently to identify the kinds of contacts needed for the successful launch of a biotechnology start-up company you can get the answers you need, including financing for your great idea, process, or tool.

WHY CARE ABOUT NETWORKING?

Chances are, when starting a biotechnology start-up company, networking is not the first thing that comes to mind as a top-priority issue. Almost by definition, a biotechnology start-up has infinite needs and limited resources. In this context, networking may seem to be a frivolous distraction at best, and something that should rightfully take a back seat to seemingly more immediate and urgent needs of the company.

At the same time, though, entrepreneurship can be a difficult and lonely path if taken alone, and no one has all the answers. Indeed, no one is expected to have all the answers. "Knowing what you don't know" will help you to appear more sophisticated as an entrepreneur to your contacts, and less risky as an investment (of time, energy, or money). Networking helps a small company avoid costly and time-consuming mistakes—both by directly identifying, or providing referrals to, free (or nearly free) resources (to make sure that you are educated about any services that a company generally has to pay for, perform due diligence before making a commitment).

If it is difficult for you to envision networking as anything but a waste of time that takes you away from the "real work," then try to think of networking as akin to a targeted research project, where the goal is to triage the immediate needs of the biotech start-up, and then to identify the ways to meet those needs. You may already know a number of the people who can help you to learn more about how to make your biotech start-up successful. The key is to be focused and targeted in identifying your objectives, individuals/companies/organizations needed to help you advance achieve your objectives, and other mechanisms to get the information you need, to help you get where you need to go.

Most of all, networking will help to identify where to put scarce resources. One of the key objectives of networking is to help differentiate between what you should be trying to accomplish on your own, and what you may need help with from others. Through active engagement in business and related social events you can gather information to help assess whether and under what circumstances it is worth paying for services—or if you should try to get them through a combination of sweat-equity, free consultations, or other means.

DEFINING EFFECTIVE NETWORKING

"Networking" generally means the development of mutually beneficial relationships for a business purpose, in this case business relationships instrumental for the growth and development of a new biotechnology start-up. Networking includes face-to-face meetings—either one-on-one or in the context of scientific societies, professional organizations, and, increasingly, digital forums and their related events. This is actually a research-intensive activity, and like any other research, effective networking requires the collection and organization of data, and the concerted use of that data to solve problems—weeding out false leads and focusing on development of productive relationships.

At its core, mutuality is critical to successful networking. This means approaching a new contact with genuine interest in his or her concerns and needs, and looking for common objectives and ways to build the relationship into more than a one-off interaction. This means that successful networking, when properly assessed, is not measured in the number of contacts, but by the range and depth of relationships formed in the process.

In essence, in reaching out to new and potential contacts, it is important to value their time and expertise as much as your own, and do everything possible to prepare for meetings and events in advance. Because you only have one opportunity to make a first impression, it is important to be as organized as possible and show respect for the time of people who you are meeting and the events and organizations behind them.

No one has all the answers; effective networking enables a nascent biotech entrepreneur to gain access to the right people with expertise with respect to financing and "doing-business" issues across the board. Done well, though, networking is neither a time-waster nor a luxury for later in the process after successful launch of the company. Rather, effective networking is a critical tool to advance the interests of your biotechnology start-up company, to meet people with the skills you need and the answers to your important questions.

This chapter provides a general overview on the kinds of communications tools that should be included in an effective networking strategy before and during the early stages of development and launch of a biotechnology start up. Effective networking helps to save time, conserve resources, and even helps identify where/when it is may be important to spend money for goods and services (rather than trying to do and learn everything yourself).

> **The Take-Away:** *Effective networking is an essential part of your business plan and may be instrumental to the success of a biotech start-up at all stages of development. Networking is not frivolous, optional and/or is not something to do only after launching your company.*

BEFORE YOU NETWORK

First impressions last; while it is not always possible to hit it off with everyone you meet, there are some important things to take into account before initiating active networking to improve chances of success.

With the goal of establishing meaningful, mutual business relationships, there are a number of preconditions for successful networking. This first section summarizes what you need to do in advance of networking and describes the tools needed to initiate a successful networking campaign. Several of these important issues are presented in greater detail in other chapters, and so are reviewed only briefly here.

1. GET A BUSINESS CARD

- The first question that someone may ask is simply whether you have a business card. Lacking a business card or—just as professionally unforgivable, running out—creates doubt in the mind of a new contact about the seriousness of your efforts. Similarly, it may not be appropriate to give out a business card from an unrelated entity, whether it is academic or otherwise, depending on the context of your meeting or discussion with potential contacts for your new company.

- The best thing is to have a business card for the new company; it does not have to be a top-of-the-line engraved card when you first get started. In fact, it is possible to order business cards online for less than $100 and to get professional results with cards delivered in a week to 10 days. For those unwilling to pry open their wallet or purse, there are printing companies that provide free cards in exchange for placing their logo on the blank side. Not an optimal solution, but the least costly. However, given the modest expenditure required, there is really no excuse not to invest in making a professional first impression on prospective contacts.

- Finally, you never know when or where you'll run into someone who could be of value, and accordingly you should never be without business cards. Some business cards should be tucked away in your wallet or purse, anywhere/anytime you venture out. Follow this simple guideline: business cards are like oxygen for a start-up company—both essential for survival.

2. PRACTICE YOUR "ELEVATOR" PITCH

- The elevator pitch is an introduction to your business that can be delivered in the length of time that it takes to take an average elevator ride with a potentially important contact. The idea is to ignite sufficient interest in your interlocutor that he/she will be open to a longer interaction to learn more about your ideas/company. A successful elevator pitch may pique the interest of a potential financial support or technical expert.

- If you don't have an elevator pitch yet, spend some time staring at your business plan, executive summary, and similar materials until you can think of the most concise, direct, interesting way to crystallize the information in 90 seconds or less.

- Practice your elevator pitch in front of a mirror until you are so comfortable with it that it becomes second nature and does not sound stilted or awkward. Practice on your friends and family. Repeat.

Some hints:

- There is little to gain from spontaneity; decide ahead of time on the best way to phrase your elevator pitch and then stick with it. It is important that the first time you hear the way something sounds it is not in the elevator with an important contact or potential colleague. The only way to avoid this is practice and sticking to your script.
- Anticipate frequently asked questions (FAQs) and write out the answers and practice them, too.
- The same guidelines apply for any oral presentation.

3. FORMALLY REGISTER/ORGANIZE YOUR COMPANY

- Before registering your new entity, invest time in choosing a name that resonates. Once you begin to successfully network it is suboptimal to rename and re-brand the company.
  i) A good name is one that sounds familiar or comfortable without actually already belonging to someone else—it is like a new article of clothing that looks and feels like you already own it without being a copy of something else already hanging in your closet. Try to avoid the annoying trends of random cApiTal letters sprinkled in, unpronounceable initials, or, worse yet, an 'X' inserted for no discernable reason.
  ii) It may be worthwhile revisiting your chosen company name to make sure you avoid names that are difficult to spell, pronounce, or already have clear or generic associations.
- Check the U.S. Patent and Trademark Office (PTO)

database to see if there are already companies with the same or similar name in your field.

- Do an Internet search to find companies in your area of specialization with the same or similar names in the United States, Europe, India and other major emerging markets, as appropriate.

- Registering your company as a Limited Liability Corporation (LLC) is generally a good way to start, as the least bureaucratic, legal organization with the fewest tax implications. Legal registration of the new company also helps to establish the formal relationship between the co-founders in cases where there is more than one scientist or a scientist and a lead business officer. It is helpful to be able to answer definitively questions about the business relationship between the cofounders, particularly where you are establishing the company with a higher profile partner.

4. REGISTER A DOMAIN NAME (OR AT LEAST GET AN EMAIL ADDRESS!)

- You can get a domain with web hosting for approximately $6-10 per month, bundled with email addresses and requiring little or no technical expertise.

- If you are not ready to commit to a domain name, or a commercial email address (e.g. www.yourdomain.com), at least set up a free email account. A free email account can be customized with the name of your company as a minimum first step for your nascent organization.

- After a few months, it is important to establish your own domain for branding purposes, and to construct a professional website for the company. Establishing a domain is greater evidence of substantial effort and investment in a biotech start-up.

5. PREPARE A NON-CONFIDENTIAL EXECUTIVE SUMMARY

- It is helpful to have a 2-3 page overview of the company and current benchmarks/milestones to use either as a leave-behind or to share later digitally;

- This should not include any business confidential or otherwise sensitive information and should by all means pass the "New York Times Test." This means that you would be proud to see any material in the non-confidential executive summary published in the New York Times.

- Frequently Asked Questions (FAQs): As noted above, you should think in advance about the kind of questions a new contact may ask to make the most out of your investment of networking time. It is really valuable to be prepared and able to answer likely questions in a way that creates confidence.

The Take Away: *Set yourself up for success before you start active networking. You can do this by answering the obvious questions before they are asked; get a business card, a domain name, a legal organization that establishes your bona fides and the relationship between you and any other founders of the company. Also be prepared when you meet a potentially important contact with a brief oral "elevator pitch," fixed answers to the most likely questions, and a brief non-confidential executive summary to use as a leave-behind.*

TREAT NETWORKING AS SERIOUSLY AS THE SCIENCE

Effective networking may be as important to the success of a new biotech start-up as a novel, innovative science platform because it may open new doors and improve access to financing and other critical assets and resources for a young enterprise. It is not a frill or a distraction. Not only that, given that a young company—like an infant—has almost limitless needs and may be extremely resource-constrained, plan a networking campaign as carefully and as seriously as preclinical research, a patent application, or any other major undertaking. Planning ahead as much as possible will help ensure targeted, useful outcomes for your networking efforts.

This requires consistent effort before and after the fact, as follows:

1. Get organized! It does not matter if the organization is paper-based or digital. Low- or high-tech can be equally effective, but some kind of organizational system for networking information is essential. It is important to decide on whether you are going to use hard-copies (i.e., binders, notebooks, etc.) to file your new contacts—or a digital system where new contacts are scanned and maintained in an electronic database, spreadsheets, etc. Maintaining organized contact lists saves time and increases exponentially the value of your networking.

2. Stay organized! It is tempting to allocate networking time primarily or exclusively to attendance of outside events and meetings, as well as collecting business cards. However, effective networking relies as much, or more, on the continuing organization and mobilization of contacts. A desk drawer full of business cards or empty binders will not serve the purpose. So the day or so after any outside meetings or events, plan to spend an hour or so either scanning new business cards or filing them in a binder by category, making notes of how and where you met a new contact, and any area of common interest.

3. Set up and maintain a calendar of events. Once you join a few online or physical organizations you may soon start to receive more invitations than you can possibly manage to attend. Review emails or paper invitations and set up a calendar and tracking system so that important opportunities don't fall in the cracks.

4. Follow-up is the key to effective networking. Initial follow up within a short time of first meeting is important to actually establish and solidify your new relationship to expand your effective network. Once you have captured

and filed information about any new contacts, follow up via a phone call, set up a digital or physical meeting, and continue to follow up. That is how a network becomes effective.

The Take Away: *It is critical to set aside significant time ahead of networking opportunities to prepare so that your networking efforts will be effective and targeted, and again in the day or week following initial meetings to file, follow-up and pursue common areas of interest with new contacts.*

PLANNING YOUR NETWORKING CAMPAIGN

1. TAKE STOCK

To make the most of your networking efforts, the first step is to assess the contacts and information you may already have. Once you figure out what you have it is easier to identify your real needs.

- Inventory your existing contacts:
  - Take a fresh look at your existing networks—any professional and personal rolodex, address books, past conference attendee lists, institutional directories, and even your kids' school directories—every address list that you have in your home and office.
  - Think about former friends and colleagues with whom you may have lost touch and with whom you may have common interests in your new venture. It is important not to overlook potentially helpful contacts, particularly in a difficult economic climate. You may also be surprised how nice it is to reconnect with people who you may not have talked to in some time, and to learn more about what they are doing. Sometimes an old contact may be useful as a bridge to a new one, either because of a company

in common or simply to remind you of a previous interest.

- Look for online resources on issues relevant to your needs. For every area of technology and at every stage of development there are online resources and tutorials. Before reaching beyond your immediate network of close friends and colleagues, educate yourself about online resources that may be available, at no charge, on issues important to you.

2. TARGET YOUR EFFORTS

- Prioritize your networking efforts based on the area of greatest immediate need(s) for the company. Gaining financial support is almost always the highest priority, and may be only one of a variety of issues where a new biotech startup needs support. Taking care of a number of housekeeping or doing-business issues first may actually make the company more attractive to potential funders. By prioritizing needs ahead of networking opportunities, and keeping your mind open to possibilities, it is more likely that you will recognize unexpected opportunities.

- Where you focus your efforts will differ depending on your area of need whether it is just information gathering, looking to hire staff or identify outside consultants, or seeking financial backing. Construct a new list specifically for your company, divided by area, and match the people you know with the needs you have.

- Following review of your existing network, you should have a good idea of where the holes are and where you need additional support. Through networking, you can build upon your network of important contacts including:

    i)   Potential business partners or financial backers

ii)   Other biotech Small and Medium Enterprises (SMEs)
iii)   Attorneys (intellectual property, corporate, or transactions [e.g., mergers and acquisitions])
iv)   Accountants/bookkeepers
v)   Staffing agencies
vi)   Incubator managers
vii)   Commercial realtors
viii) Consultants (regulatory affairs, management strategy, etc.)

Many of them will not only know people you should know—further expanding your knowledge base—but they will also have their finger on the pulse of the local biotechnology community. They are the "canaries in the coal mine;" that is, they are the predictors and harbingers of economic activity.

For example, attorneys are needed to set up a biotechnology company as a legal entity, and so their level of activity directly relates to the level of entrepreneurship taking place. Accountants are also in this category, since few scientists or medical researchers are capable of generating financial reports and projects. If firms are growing, then they are hiring, and staffing agencies are busy. If firms are growing, then they are out-growing their space, perhaps leaving start-up space in an incubator and working with commercial realtors to secure larger offices and research/manufacturing facilities.

3. MORE ON IDENTIFYING PRIORITIES FOR NETWORKING

After identifying the gaps in your network, actively seek to fill in those gaps. As always, follow up with new contacts to establish and solidify the nascent business relationship. Priority areas likely include:

- Finance issues: Not just funding, but also financial management (accounting, taxes, internal auditing, required annual reports and submissions to regulatory authorities).
- Legal support: Among the range of issues that you may

need to educate yourself about include the appropriate form of legal organization for the company, how to protect commercially valuable intellectual property—including patents, trademarks, or undisclosed data (trade secrets). The size of the law firm is a minor factor in your decision-making. If it is a larger practice, find one that will value your small business and be willing to grow with it. If a smaller practice, find one that still contains expertise during the later stages of patent prosecution, such as National Phase filing (deciding in which countries to seek patent protection). Find a law firm with core expertise in biotechnology, in which the attorneys who would work with you have formal education in the life sciences. Also, take into account that these are people with whom you may end up spending a lot of time and who may ask for a great deal of your money. Choose carefully and don't be afraid to reassess after some months to see whether you are comfortable with your choice.

- Developing/improving your executive summary or business plan: If you do not yet have a fully developed executive summary or business plan, then one of the first deliverables for your networking should be to identify the resources needed for writing an effective business plan. This process also helps to find the strengths and weaknesses in your planning, including development of benchmarks for investors. Other bio-entrepreneurs may be one of your best resources for discussing a variety of business-related issues, such as how to develop or improve an executive summary or full-blown business plan.

- Information technology (IT) and website: A fully-fledged website is not essential to start networking. However, a well-designed website is an extremely effective tool both to provide a portal for providing in-depth information about the company, and build credibility as to the seriousness of the effort. If the company does not have a website, one of the higher level needs is to identify an affordable design and platform for your company website, and ongoing IT needs. Many universities and art schools have programs in web design. Your company may be an attractive project, at little or no cost, to an aspiring/recent graduate student in need of a reference and accomplishments on their resume.

- Design: Design is an often under-appreciated asset that helps a small start-up company project an image of success. Developing a logo and design projects as professional an image as possible for an early-stage company. As mentioned above, universities and art schools are valid paths to explore for the entrepreneur.

- Contract research organizations (CROs) and contract manufacturing organizations (CMOs). Such consultants provide services beyond the skill sets of the entrepreneur and likely other founders. For CROs, an example would be preclinical testing of a compound's toxicity. For CMOs, an example would be coming up with a "recipe" for the compound readily transferable from animal to human studies.

- Grant opportunities from the U.S. or foreign governments, as appropriate.

- Private foundations. Venture philanthropy, the funding of for-profits by non-profits, is an increasingly important source to tap into for capital.

- Other pre-clinical and clinical research services, such as regulatory consultants well-versed in dealing with enforcement agencies such as the U.S. Food and Drug Administration (FDA).

The Take Away: *Identify the gaps in your network for focused work to broaden or deepen contacts in critical areas. Review and prioritize networking needs on a regular basis. When the right people cross your path* *you will be ready with the right questions.*

NETWORKING TOOLS AND RESOURCES

1. FREE OR NEARLY SO

Identify as many free networking opportunities as possible. These include:

- Digital media: Invest time in developing a meaningful online profile and take an active role in managing your network by joining groups and finding old and new contacts in areas of interest. Try to increase interest in your own website, blogging, or other efforts relating to your company through online networking outlets. Some of the most popular for business include:

  i)   LinkedIn: http://www.linkedin.com/home
  ii) FaceBook: http://www.facebook.com/login.php
  iii) Plaxo: http://www.plaxo.com/
  iv) Twitter: http://twitter.com/

- Your own company website: At a cost of only $6-10 per month for web-hosting, a basic website for your new company is an important avenue for nearly free networking. Though many web-hosting services provide some do-it-yourself services, it is best to pay for a professional looking website. There is no other source of information about your biotech start-up that give you complete control, and that is available online for interested contacts to review anytime, anywhere. By the same token, it is very important that your website contain accurate, reliable, and timely information. So once you make a commitment to establish a website, take that commitment seriously.

- University/research institution associations and organizations: Your current institution, or the one from which your core technology was obtained. Your current or most recent research institution has—or will know of—entrepreneurial resources available through the technology transfer office, licensing office, or other related organization. In a multi-disciplinary university, it may also be possible to access resources from the departments of economics, business, law, etc.

- Alumni organizations (both your alma mater and any other prior academic/research affiliations): Reconnect with colleagues from previous academic institutions, encompassing and relating to your own studies and mentors. Many colleges and universities now also offer online networking, to supplement their regular opportunities to meet in-person with alumni and related industry professionals.

- Companies: A large part of the DNA of biotechnology start-ups in the United States, and the reason for continuing American pre-eminence in the sector, is the mobility of alumni large and small pharmaceutical and bio-pharmaceutical companies alike. Scientists who have worked for or consulted with one or more companies should start with the workplace as an important source of contacts, and also look into other spin-off companies for additional contacts.

- Public seminars and other free or low-cost events: Sponsored by local, state, or national governmental organizations, research institutes, and/ or professional associations. For example, law firms often sponsor speakers culled from their ranks as a marketing and outreach tool. A related opportunity to be on the look-out for is staffing/volunteer opportunities with professional groups that may provide sweat-equity opportunities to help organize or otherwise attend relevant industry events.

- Venues specifically designed for start-ups: As noted, research institutes, universities, incubators, and related organizations, may provide mentoring and support through the technology transfer office or other support services. University incubator centers or other SME support may also be available locally.

2. NETWORKING TOOLS THAT COST MONEY

You should be able to tell when it is important to move beyond free or low-cost networking tools and how to tell the difference between a valuable service and a come-on. Programs or organizations you may want to consider include:

- "Biotech Boot-camps": In most major metropolitan areas of the U.S., you are likely within 50-100 miles of a "biotech boot-camp" taking place several times a year. If you are at the start of your journey in commercial biotechnology, it may be worth attending an intensive one-to-three-day boot-camp to cover the basic elements of establishing a SME and related doing-business issues for an ongoing enterprise. Through attendance at a biotech boot-camp, you will also likely gain access to continuing support and online resources – starting with the "faculty" and organizers.
- Professional associations and memberships: State-wide biotechnology trade councils, national associations such as the Biotechnology Industry Organization (BIO), regional and local as well as women's biotech groups (e.g. Women in Bio, Women Entrepreneurs in Science and Technology), or other specialized organizations.

These organizations may have focused committees, work areas, or events for your company or area of interest. In particular, the BIO annual meeting provides particular opportunities for academics, translational research and SMEs.

The Take Away: *There will be networking opportunities that are not free and worth paying the price for admission. Before considering these, be sure to exhaust all of the free/low-cost resources available in your per-*

*sonal network, university/research institution/compa-
ny, and own community.*

FUNDAMENTAL RULES OF ATTRACTION

In every interaction, the basic fundamentals remain the same. No matter how positive the initial meeting, successful networking relies on persistent follow-up and timely completion of whatever deliverable is discussed during the first meeting or conversation. Doing your homework before any meeting or event homework before the event includes research on likely participants and attendees and materials you need to share. The same is true in preparation for a cold call or any other unsolicited approaches. Your chances of success are greater if you take the time to learn as much as possible about the other person, affiliated company, or related technology of greatest common interest.

1. BEFORE THE EVENT: WHO WILL BE THERE?

- Participants: How much can you find out about who will be there? Get and review the list of participants and their biographic data; if unavailable beforehand, then take time at the start of the event to look for a list of participants and identify a few potential contacts of potentially greatest interest to get you started.
- Learn something about the organization and the event itself. Even if it is your first time attending, be sure that you have educated yourself about the mission and activities of the group.
- One-to-one networking opportunities: Find out if there is any opportunity to set up one-on-one meetings ahead of time. Reach out directly by email or phone to the potential contact or via the event coordinator.

2. WHAT TO BRING

Be prepared to make a great impression and get others excited about your endeavor. Be ready with your business card and elevator pitch.

It may also be helpful to bring the one-to-two-page non-confidential executive summary that you have prepared in advance to use as a leave-behind for interested colleagues. Nonetheless, it is important to be judicious in deciding to whom you give more than a card. Remember that you can also follow up by email to send more information. It is always better to say less than more. In this context, it is helpful to practice your introduction and talking points ahead of the event.

3. AT THE EVENT: MAKE THE MOST OF EACH OPPORTUNITY

- As you enter the room, take a look around and see if there is anyone there who you already know. If not, don't let that worry you, as many others will likely be in the same situation. First and foremost, remember to always smile and make eye contact when you introduce yourself. Repeat the name of each person you meet and look straight at them to help reinforce it. This will get easier over time and with practice. So, just keep trying if it does not come naturally.

- Follow your plan—use your elevator pitch, stick to the subject, and avoid irrelevant, potentially sensitive topics. Be sure to limit your initial questions to the person's primary area of expertise. Furthermore, try to circulate and talk to a number of new people, spending 5-10 minutes with each new contact—then moving on. If there is someone particularly interesting, there is no harm in letting him or her know that you hope to reconnect later in the event or else to follow up afterwards by phone or email. When you meet someone of little interest and relevance, it is not imperative that you spend a lot of time with them. As long as you are courteous, you may limit the encounter. You can say something along the lines of, "I know you've got a lot of people to meet; I don't want to keep you." Others, like you, are there to maximize their time and efforts.

- It may be obvious, but worth reinforcing, that it is

best not to drink or eat to excess, or even to try to carry a plate and drink around with you if avoidable (networking can be fattening, but it does not have to be). Play it safe by starting with something non-alcoholic and go from there.

- Also, it is important to respect boundaries; try not to interrupt what looks like a private conversation. Look for the right moment, or wait for another opportunity if someone does not look like they want to be approached or is in the midst of another conversation. Don't be too concerned if your first few outings for the new company are a little challenging. As with other new pursuits, getting good at networking requires practice and concerted effort. Persistence is the key to building your network and to overall success. It should also get to be at least a little fun over time as you build your network.

The take away: *With practice, you will become more comfortable with face-to-face networking, approaching strangers or near-strangers, and making new contacts. Like any skill, this requires practice. You will maximize your return on investment in networking time by: 1) preparing ahead of the event, 2) learning about the organization and the specific meeting, 3) exploring who will be there, and, most importantly, 4) working on your own preparatory materials and introductory remarks.*

ENDS AND MEANS: SOME CLOSING THOUGHTS

It is worth repeating that networking is a means to an end and not an end in and of itself. Effective networking will help you to expand contacts to make the most of scarce resources (time, money, staff, etc.) either before launch of a start-up or in the early phases.

The biggest issue for start-ups is the tradeoff between time and money. Networking can help you to figure out what you should try to be doing on your own and what you should pay others for in terms of goods and services.

In networking, as in any other area, measurable benchmarks are important to establish metrics and evaluate progress towards goals.

The good news is that, with organization and concerted effort, anyone can develop an extensive network that will greatly improve the odds of success – whether that means getting the early funding needed to launch a company, finding the right partner to lead the business or science side of an enterprise, or the appropriate process, service provider, or lab equipment.

In conclusion, unless you are a successful, serial bio-entrepreneur with well-established resources and contacts, networking is essential. And chances are, the most successful bio-entrepreneurs continue to add to and refresh their networks. So, get out there, breathe deeply, and turn strangers into colleagues and advocates.

You cannot let your work speak for itself. If you do, your work will be mute!

About the Editor

Michael L. Salgaller, PhD, has over 20 years of business and scientific and business experience in various life science sectors. He is an experienced industry and venture capital executive with a successful background in business development, strategic planning, technology assessment, and capital formation. He has held various positions with consulting and drug discovery firms, as well as directing the development of cancer therapeutics. He began his career as a senior staff scientist at the National Institutes of Health, and has consulted for various biotech companies, economic development entities, and disease foundations. Dr. Salgaller earned his PhD in pathology from the Ohio State University, and was awarded a biotechnology fellowship at the National Cancer Institute. He is an author on over 60 articles and book chapters, and serves on the editorial boards of several journals. He was elected to the Sigma Xi Research Honorary, as well as the Pi Delta Epsilon Journalism Honorary.

Michael can be contacted at *mlsalgaller@yahoo.com.*

Related Titles from Logos Press®

http://www.logos-press.com

Building Biotechnology
Scientists know science; businesspeople know business. This book explains both.

Hardcover ISBN: 978-09734676-5-9
Softcover ISBN: 978-09734676-6-6

Best Practices in Biotechnology Business Development
Valuation, Licensing, Cash Flow, Pharmacoeconomics, Market Selection, Communication, and Intellectual Property

ISBN: 978-09734676-0-4

Building the Case for Biotechnology
Management Case Studies in Science, Laws, Regulations, Politics, and Business

Hardcover ISBN: 978-1-934899-16-8
Softcover ISBN: 978-1-934899-15-1